HERMES BOOKS

John Herington, General Editor

Also available in this series:

OVID

SARA MACK

YALE UNIVERSITY PRESS
NEW HAVEN AND LONDON

Designed by Sally Harris
and set in Palatino type by
Brevis Press, Bethany, Connecticut.
Printed in the United States of America by
Vail-Ballou Press, Binghamton, New York.

Library of Congress Cataloging-in-Publication Data

Mack, Sara, 1939–
  Ovid.

  (Hermes books)
  Bibliography: p.
  Includes index.
  I. Ovid, 43 B.C.–17 or 18 A.D.—Criticism and
interpretation. I. Title.
PA6537.M23 1988   871'.01   87–37157
ISBN 0–300–04294–9 (alk. paper)
ISBN 0–300–04295–7 (pbk. : alk. paper)

The paper in this book meets the guidelines for
permanence and durability of the Committee on
Production Guidelines for Book Longevity
of the Council on Library Resources.

10 9 8 7 6 5 4 3 2 1

CONTENTS

FOREWORD

"IT WOULD BE A PITY," SAID NIETZSCHE, "IF THE CLASSICS should speak to us less clearly because a million words stood in the way." His forebodings seem now to have been realized. A glance at the increasing girth of successive volumes of the standard journal of classical bibliography, *L'Année Philologique*, since World War II is enough to demonstrate the proliferation of writing on the subject in our time. Unfortunately, the vast majority of the studies listed will prove on inspection to be largely concerned with points of detail and composed by and for academic specialists in the field. Few are addressed to the literate but nonspecialist adult or to that equally important person, the intelligent but uninstructed beginning student; and of those few, very few indeed are the work of scholars of the first rank, equipped for their task not merely with raw classical erudition but also with style, taste, and literary judgment.

It is a strange situation. On one side stand the classical masters of Greece and Rome, those models of concision, elegance, and understanding of the human condition, who composed least of all for narrow technologists, most of all for the Common Reader (and, indeed, the Common Hearer). On the other side stands a sort of industrial complex, processing those masters into an annually growing output of technical articles and monographs. What is lacking, it seems, in our society as well as in our scholarship, is the kind of book that was supplied for earlier generations by such men as Richard

Jebb and Gilbert Murray in the intervals of their more technical researches—the kind of book that directed the general reader not to the pyramid of secondary literature piled over the burial places of the classical writers but to the living faces of the writers themselves, as perceived by a scholar-humanist with a deep knowledge of, and love for, his subject. Not only for the sake of the potential student of classics, but also for the sake of the humanities as a whole, within and outside academe, it seems that this gap in classical studies ought to be filled. The Hermes series is a modest attempt to fill it.

We have sought men and women possessed of a rather rare combination of qualities: a love for literature in other languages, extending into modern times; a vision that extends beyond academe to contemporary life itself; and above all an ability to express themselves in clear, lively, and graceful English, without polysyllabic language or parochial jargon. For the aim of the series requires that they should communicate to nonspecialist readers, authoritatively and vividly, their personal sense of why a given classical author's writings have excited people for centuries and why they can continue to do so. Some are classical scholars by profession, some are not; each has lived long with the classics, and especially with the author about whom he or she writes in this series.

The first, middle, and last goal of the Hermes series is to guide the general reader to a dialogue with the classical masters rather than to acquaint him or her with the present state of scholarly research. Thus our volumes contain few or no footnotes; even within the texts, references to secondary literature are kept to a minimum. At the end of each volume, however, is a short bibliography that includes recommended English translations, and selected literary criticism, as well as historical and (when appropriate) biographical studies. Throughout, all quotations from the Greek or Latin texts are given in English translation.

In these ways we hope to let the classics speak again, with a minimum of modern verbiage (as Nietzsche wished), to the widest possible audience of interested people.

John Herington

PREFACE

My spirit is moved to sing of shapes changed
into new bodies. Gods, inspire my undertaking
(for you have changed it too).

[*Metamorphoses* 1.1–3]

OVID BEGINS HIS GREAT POEM ABOUT CHANGE WITH A SUGGES-
tion that the poem's form changed even as he wrote it. It
should, therefore, be no surprise that my book about the *Meta-*
morphoses has undergone a transformation. The book I meant
to write when I received a fellowship at the National Human-
ities Center was a scholarly study of Ovid's narrative tech-
nique in the *Metamorphoses*, addressed to an audience of
professional Classicists. What emerged instead was this vol-
ume, an introduction to all of the poems of Ovid, intended
for the general reader. Both books, the one that might have
been and the one that is, began to take shape at the Human-
ities Center and neither could have come into being (since, as
the poet Lucretius knew full well, nothing can come from
nothing) without that year of undisturbed reading, thinking,
talking, and writing (not to mention the superb library ser-
vice). The Center, with its peculiar blend of monastic isolation
and shipboard conviviality, was a perfect setting for Ovidian
thoughts.

When I began to write I did not intend to include any
Latin in the book. A little Latin crept in anyway despite my
efforts, but I have translated all that is there, as well as all

that is not there, and most of the time I made Ovid speak in English. The translations are my own, not especially elegant, but as clear and as close to the Latin as I could get without contorting the English language too much.

My debt to other scholars is enormous, even though only a few could be mentioned in the brief bibliography at the end of the volume.

I OVID TODAY

Wherever Roman power extends in conquered lands, I
shall be on people's lips; in fame through all the ages—
if poets' prophecies have any truth in them—I shall
live.

SO WROTE THE POET OVID, OR, TO GIVE HIM HIS PROPER ROMAN
name, Publius Ovidius Naso, in about A.D. 8, as he completed
his greatest poem, the *Metamorphoses*. *Vivam* ("I shall live")
he concluded proudly, and indeed he does live, even though
Roman power has long since waned and Latin is no longer a
"living" language. From the time his first poems appeared in
the 20s B.C. until now Ovid has been a favorite with most
readers, for he is both human and humane, and his subjects
are of timeless interest: love, sex, friendship, the relation be-
tween man and gods, the individual and the state, art and
life, words and things. He was immensely popular in his own
day:

> For although our age has produced great poets, fame has
> not been grudging to my genius, and though I put many
> ahead of myself I am said to be not less than they, and I
> am read most of all throughout the world.
>
> [125–28]

These verses come from *Tristia* 4.10, one of the poems Ovid
wrote late in life after he had been exiled and his books
banned from public libraries. Selections from his works were
even performed on stage during his lifetime, "often danced
for the people," he claims in *Tristia* 2.519. Graffiti scrawled

1

on walls in Pompeii quoting (or sometimes misquoting) his verses show that people knew parts of his work more or less by heart in the first century A.D.

That Ovid's works survived the early Christian period despite their themes—which include seduction, adultery, and incest, besides those just mentioned—attests to their popularity with ordinary readers. Later admirers include a ninth-century bishop (Theodulf of Orleans), Peter Abelard, the famous twelfth-century philosopher and theologian, a thirteenth-century pope (Innocent III), and Martin Luther, who found time to read Ovid as well as to reform the church. Ovid was one of Milton's three favorite authors, Wordsworth (as he comments in a note to his "Ode to Lycoris") was "quite in a passion whenever I found him, in books of criticism, placed below Virgil," and Stendhal decided "that it could be pleasant to know Latin, which had been my punishment for so many years" when he discovered Ovid (*Vie de Henri Brulard* [1835], chap. 10).

I shall say something about Ovid's vast influence on the European arts in chapter 6. Here I would like to look at some qualities of his poetry that make him especially appealing to a late twentieth-century audience. Readers today may not be better equipped to appreciate Ovid than was a Renaissance or an eighteenth-century audience, but we are certainly more in tune with Ovid's manner and interests than were Victorian and earlier twentieth-century readers. In those generations it was widely assumed that literature had to be "serious" to be good. Consequently Ovid was often dismissed by scholars as trivial. Most of us were taught to regard the Romans as very sober, very grave writers who lacked a sense of humor and had little joie de vivre. (The high school Latin curriculum in most schools still reflects this assumption, and it remains what it has been for generations: Caesar's *Gallic Wars*, Cicero's *Catilinarians*, and Vergil's *Aeneid*, all very fine works, all very sober works.) Ovid, who does not fit the mold, is seldom taught in high school and not as often as he deserves in college and graduate school. He shows us a side of Roman character that students raised on Roman patriotic legend and on readings from Caesar, Cicero, and Vergil do not generally meet: high spirits and a sense of fun. Today we are prepared by our experiences in the theater and by our reading to expect meaning as well as entertainment in comedy. We are ready for Ovid.

Ovid's fascination with the human condition and the human psyche is also akin to ours. The drives, tensions, and self-deceptions that make up what we today call psychology— who is more keenly aware of these than Ovid? The *Ars Amatoria*, or *Art of Love*, for all the cynicism of its speaker, has a great deal to say about relationships between men and women. The *Metamorphoses* is full of portraits of people we know. Which of us has not been bored to death by a Nestor relating his "exploits"? Even though there is no "Phaëthon complex" named after Ovid's teenager who tries to drive the horses of his father, the Sun, destroying himself and nearly burning up the world in the process, we are all familiar with the phenomenon of sons trying to prove their worth (and their identity) by competing with their fathers. Psychology recognizes the attraction a daughter may feel toward her father as much as that of a boy toward his mother, even though it labels it "Electra complex" rather than "Myrrha complex." And which of us has not gone through something like Myrrha's emotional turmoil as we persuaded ourselves to a course we knew was wrong? Some of Ovid's portraits in the *Metamorphoses* are practically case-studies of abnormal personalities. It would be difficult to find a clearer instance of total self-absorption than in Ovid's account of Narcissus, who falls in love with his own image and wastes away in *Metamorphoses* 3.

Nowhere in literature are there more penetrating studies

of female psychology than in the *Heroides*. Even Dryden, who found flaws in Ovid's wit, went to his writings to study the passions. In the ancient world only Euripides can match Ovid in his interest in and knowledge of women. Who but Ovid would have composed fifteen letters from women of Greek mythology to their menfolk giving a woman's perspective on what had always been presented from a man's point of view? What, in Ovid's rendering, the slave Briseis sees and feels when she is taken away from Achilles and handed over to Agamemnon has little to do with what Agamemnon and Achilles think the issues are. And Ovid sees, as Euripides saw before him, that Hermione is what she is largely because she had Helen for a mother. It would be bad enough to have the most beautiful woman of all time for one's mother (mother-daughter relations are difficult, at best), but when that mother not only owns the face that launched a thousand ships but also abandoned the daughter when she did so, psychological problems are obviously in store. Ovid's insights into such matters as these are rarely surpassed.

We are much less embarrassed by Ovid's references to sexual matters than were our parents and our grandparents. We need not be put off, as they were, or irrelevantly titillated by his occasional sexual explicitness and his typical sexual suggestiveness. And Ovid should appeal enormously to the generation that has fought to make equal rights a reality. No one but Ovid would have written two thousand years ago that sexual satisfaction should be equal for both partners, that sex was no good if the woman acquiesced because it was her duty. Not for him the woman who submits to the man while thinking about her spinning! Nor for him the prostitute. Why, he asks, should one partner get paid for what both partners should enjoy?

Both modern experience and modern criticism have made us better able to evaluate Ovid's ready shifts from pose to pose and his worldly cynicism. We are more likely today than earlier readers were to distinguish between the poetic persona, or "mask," that a poet creates for himself in his poems and the historical poet. Thus we can enjoy the different poses Ovid tries on in the *Amores* without being bothered by inconsistencies in attitude and being worried about whether he is "sincere." We can likewise enjoy the urbane worldliness and occasional cynicism of the professor of love who thinks he has love down to a science (but clearly has not) without accepting his premises as ours or as the historical Ovid's. Like Catullus before him, Ovid warned his readers not to confuse the poet *in* the poem with the man who wrote the poem, claiming that his life was pure while his Muse was licentious (*Tristia* 2.353–56). Readers brought up to read a poet's biography in his poetry have not always listened.

Ovid's narrative techniques, again, look forward to twentieth-century developments in fiction. All of us today have been raised on fiction; most of us have probably read more novels than any other kind of literature and are likely to be sensitive to Ovid's continual experimentation with narrative technique. Even if we do not read the critical literature about novels, we have read enough fiction to be aware of the different ways a story can be told, the importance of the narrator or narrators, and the various effects that can be achieved by presenting the same story from different perspectives. Ovid was interested in these problems long before such terms as "point of view" or "reader-response" criticism were invented.

Ovid's very modern-seeming treatment of the story of Orpheus and Eurydice in the *Metamorphoses* is a good example of his sophisticated narrative technique. About forty years earlier, Vergil had included a moving version of the story in his *Georgics,* and Ovid uses this as the starting point for his own astonishingly different version. Compare Vergil's opening with Ovid's:

illa quidem, dum te fugeret per flumina praeceps,
immanem ante pedes hydram moritura puella
servantem ripas alta non vidit in herba.
at chorus aequalis Dryadum clamore supremos
implevit montis; flerunt Rhodopeiae arces
altaque Pangaea et Rhesi Mavortia tellus
atque Getae atque Hebrus et Actias Orithyia.
ipse cava solans aegrum testudine amorem
te, dulcis coniunx, te solo in litore secum,
te veniente die, te decedente canebat.
Taenarias etiam fauces, alta ostia Ditis,
et caligantem nigra formidine lucum
ingressus. . . .

                                               [*Geo.* 4.457–69]

But she [Eurydice] trying to get away from you [Aristaeus] was running along the river as fast as she could, doomed girl, and did not see an enormous snake hiding in the tall grass along the river bank before her feet. A band of Dryads of her own age filled the mountaintops with their cries. The heights of Rhodope wept, and lofty Pangaea and Rhesus's martial land and the Getans and the Hebrus and Attic Orithyia. But Orpheus, solacing his anguished love with his lyre, sang of you, sweet wife— of you he sang to himself on the lonely shore, of you he sang as day arrived, of you as day departed. He even entered hell's jaws, the lofty entrance to the house of Dis, the grove dark with fear.

exitus auspicio gravior. nam nupta per herbas
dum nova naiadum turba comitata vagatur,
occidit in talum serpentis dente recepto.
quam satis ad superas postquam Rhodopeius auras
deflevit vates, ne non temptaret et umbras,
ad Styga Taenaria est ausus descendere porta

perque leves populos simulacraque functa sepulcro
Persephonen adiit inamoenaque regna tenentem
umbrarum dominum. . . .

[*Meta.* 10.8–16]

The outcome of the wedding was worse than the omens
that inaugurated it; for, while the new bride was wan-
dering through the grass, accompanied by a crowd of
Naiads, she died, having received a serpent's tooth in
her ankle. When he had mourned her enough to the
breezes above, the Thracian bard thought he'd try the
shades as well, and dared to descend to the Styx by the
Spartan entrance; through the insubstantial nations, the
ghostly images of those who had received burial, he ap-
proached Persephone and the lord of the shades who
rules an unlovely kingdom.

Every detail of Vergil's lines is chosen for its emotional effect:
the girl running, the enormous snake hidden in the grass, the
pathetic epithet "doomed to die" (*moritura*), while the hideous
death itself is left to our imaginations, the sympathetic reac-
tion of nature and finally the fourfold repetition of "you" (*te*),
as Orpheus sings his unceasing lament. In Ovid's version, by
contrast, no detail seems chosen for emotional effect. The nar-
rator seems to be quite uninterested in engaging his reader
in the story. The passage is introduced by "for" (*nam*), one of
the least pathetic conjunctions available in Latin (and in En-
glish); Eurydice's death occurs abruptly—"she drops dead"
(*occidit*). Even minor rewriting could have improved the effect.
Occidit could have been delayed to create a moment of sus-
pense and thus of interest: "in talum serpentis dente recepto /
occidit" (having received a serpent's tooth in the ankle, she
died). Instead Ovid kills Eurydice first, then adds the ser-
pent's tooth to explain the fact of her death. Orpheus's re-
action to his wife's loss is equally unemotional and unmoving.

A literal translation would be "whom enough when the bard had mourned." *Satis* (enough) seems to me to be at once too specific and not specific enough. How much, it invites us to ask, is enough? Furthermore, "in order not to not try the shades as well" (a more literal translation of *ne non temptaret et umbras* than my translation above) is a very offhand way of introducing the momentous decision to undergo death in order to win Eurydice's release. The narrator has no burning interest in penetrating the mind of his subject.

Ovid goes on in more or less the same vein throughout the passage. When Orpheus forgets the prohibition against looking back at Eurydice as she follows him out of the Underworld, and he loses her a second time, this time forever, Ovid tries to find an analogy for Orpheus's horror through a sequence of similes drawn from the obscurest imaginable legends:

> Orpheus was stupefied by the double death of his wife in just the same way as the frightened man who saw the three necks of the dog, the middle one with a chain on it, whose terror did not leave him until his former nature did, as rock grew up over his body; or as Olenus was who wanted to seem guilty and took the charge on himself, and you, unhappy Lethaea who had too much pride in your own beauty—two hearts that beat as one, now stones on damp Mt. Ida.
>
> [*Meta.* 10.64–71]

The similes would, I am sure, have been no more illuminating to a Roman reader than they are to us; they only obfuscate. Perhaps Ovid's most outrageous addition to the story is his cool assertion that Orpheus gave up associating with women after Eurydice's death and introduced pederasty among the Thracians. Orpheus was the "author" or "inventor" (*auctor*) of the practice, says he, as if it were a notable achievement, using the word the Romans were fond of attributing to the founder of a colony or the inventor of a new kind of poetry. Why does Ovid tell the story in this peculiar way? Some will say that he was not capable of Vergilian pathos, which is doubtless true, but he shows in his account of Ceyx and Alcyone that follows what he could have done with his Orpheus, had he chosen to. Why does he do it then? Partly, I am sure, to avoid trying to do what Vergil excelled at and had already done, and also, I think (and if I am right, Ovid is being very modern indeed), to add a new dimension to the story by the way he tells it. The rest of Book 10, after Orpheus's failed attempt to rescue Eurydice from death, is given over to Orpheus, the archetypal musician who can draw nature to listen to his song. And the song is a miniature *Metamorphoses* in which Orpheus sings his own sequence of songs, including one about Pygmalion, who carves an ivory statue that comes alive, one about Myrrha's incestuous love for her father, and one about Venus's love for Myrrha's son, Adonis—just to name the longest songs. When the main narrator returns in Book 11 to conclude Orpheus's story, he seems to have changed his attitude to his character and thus our attitude to the story. No longer is he distant and uninvolved. He now takes an active role in creating sympathy for his character. He editorializes in a rather Vergilian way about the madness of the Maenads who kill Orpheus. He exclaims in horror as the poet who could hold animals and rocks in thrall cannot save himself from the hands of frenzied women. He describes the poet's death with a simile designed to involve us emotionally in the scene: the Maenads are compared to a pack of birds mobbing an owl out by mistake in the daylight; Orpheus is like a stag pitted against a pack of dogs in the arena. The poet addresses Orpheus in pity:

> te maestae volucres, Orpheu, te turba ferarum,
> te rigidi silices, tua carmina saepe secutae

fleverunt silvae; positis te frondibus arbor
tonsa comas luxit.

[Meta. 11.44–47]

Grieving birds wept for you, Orpheus, for you crowds of
animals mourned, and rigid rocks and trees that often
followed your song; the trees shed their tresses in mourn-
ing for you.

Ovid seems again to be alluding to Vergil, to the lines I quoted
earlier, where "you" was repeated four times as the poet
mourned with Orpheus for Eurydice. Ovid may well be show-
ing, as he so often does, that he can outdo Vergil by adding
a fifth clause (four "you" clauses, and one "your" clause) but
this time he is not undercutting, this time he is not under-
mining the pathos—in fact the first two and a half lines could
almost have been written by Vergil. If Ovidian humor peeps
out in the last of the five clauses, as the tree sheds its leaves
for Orpheus, it still does not spoil the emotional effect. And
finally the narrator creates a satisfying, romantic happy end-
ing after Orpheus's dismemberment. His shade goes off to
the Underworld to find Eurydice in the Fields of the Blessed.
Now that he is dead he can safely look back at Eurydice when-
ever he likes. Orpheus embraces Eurydice as Aeneas wanted
to embrace Creusa in Aeneid 2 and Anchises in Aeneid 6 but
could not, for they were dead and he was not. Dead Orpheus
holds dead Eurydice "in his eager arms."

 How are we to explain this change in the narrator's at-
titude toward his character? Could it be that Orpheus, as he
sang his song in Book 10, won over his own narrator, his own
creator? In the course of Orpheus's song his attitude to Myrrha
changes from initial hostility to sympathy; Pygmalion, in Or-
pheus's song, falls in love with and so brings to life the statue
he has created. Perhaps Orpheus's creator, the poet narrator
we call Ovid, has fallen under the spell of Orpheus's song

and thus animated his own creation in the same way. If this reading is right Ovid has set foot on the road that leads to Chaucer, to Fielding and Sterne, and on to twentieth-century experiments with multiple narrators and varied narrative perspectives. At the least, Ovid, seeing different possibilities in the story of Orpheus and Eurydice from those Vergil had seen, uses the power of his words to make an old story new.

Ovid lives indeed, as he said he would at the end of the *Metamorphoses*, and he seems to reach out from his century to ours. Reading him in Latin is best, of course. Many reluctant students forced to take Latin in school have come later to agree with Stendhal that it was worth learning the language in order to read Ovid. Anyone who knows even a little Latin should enjoy reading Ovid in the Loeb Library edition, which has facing Latin and English texts. I urge all readers to have a text of some kind handy as they go along. I have kept quotations to a minimum—just enough, I hope, to make people want to reach for Ovid's work itself.

II OVID IN HIS
OWN TIME

MUCH OF THE INFORMATION WE HAVE ABOUT OVID'S LIFE
comes from his autobiographical *Tristia* 4.10. There we learn
something about his family, his friends, and his contacts with
other poets of the day: he had a brother exactly one year older
than himself, he had two brief, unsatisfactory marriages be-
fore marrying the woman to whom he was apparently still
devoted at his death, Propertius read his elegies to him, Ovid
"heard" Horace but only "saw" Vergil. Much of what Ovid
wrote in *Tristia* 4.10, like the facts mentioned above, has the
ring of truth. It is likely to be somewhat fictionalized as is any
poem (or anything written, for that matter), but much of what
he tells us in the poem fits with what we know otherwise.
The passage gives us a much clearer sense of Ovid than we
have of other Roman poets for whom we have only late and
rather fanciful *Lives*.

In this chapter I shall try to give an idea of the range and
nature of Ovid's work and to provide the reader with a brief
introduction to the individual poems. Because his *Amores*,
Heroides, *Ars Amatoria*, and *Metamorphoses* have been most in-
fluential over the centuries and are most accessible to the
Latinless and nonspecialist reader, these are the poems I shall
concentrate on in the rest of the book. Here I shall emphasize
the less well known poems, in particular the *Fasti* and the
poems from exile (the *Tristia* and the *Epistulae ex Ponto*), but I
shall include brief accounts of the others, each in its proper
chronological place (to the extent that our inadequate infor-

mation about dates of composition allows us to determine it). Anyone who is especially interested in one of the poems that receives scant attention here might want to move directly on to chapter 3 or 4 for fuller discussion before returning to this survey.

Publius Ovidius Naso was born in Sulmo (modern Sulmona) about ninety miles east and slightly north of Rome on March 20, 43 b.c. This was one year after the assassination of Julius Caesar, less than a year before the execution of the great orator Cicero, and twelve years before the Battle of Actium, the battle that put an end to decades of civil war with the defeat of Antony and Cleopatra by Caesar's grandnephew Octavian (Gaius Iulius Caesar Octavianus), the future emperor Augustus. Ovid was born into a fairly wealthy family of equestrian rank, the sort of family that expected its sons to follow a political career—that is, to hold a succession of increasingly important offices in Italy and abroad. Ovid and his brother were educated first in Sulmo and then sent to Rome to finish their schooling, which in their day emphasized the study of rhetoric and public speaking, essential for law and politics, the two most acceptable professions for a man of good family. Ovid had been interested in poetry from an early age, even though his father, like many fathers since, had reservations about his son's pursuing such a precarious profession:

> Often my father said, why try a useless task? Homer himself had no money to leave!
>
> [Tr. 4.10.21–22]

Yet whenever the boy tried to write prose, he tells us:

> A poem would come, of its own accord, into the right meter, and what I tried to say ended up in verse.
>
> [25–26]

Or, as Alexander Pope put it centuries later, "I lisp'd in Numbers, for the Numbers came" (*An Epistle to Dr. Arbuthnot,* line 128).

After they had completed their education, the Naso brothers did what was expected of them and ran for office, the brother enthusiastically, Ovid reluctantly. Ovid's brother died when he was only twenty, and Ovid, after holding a minor office or two, found that life in the "wordy forum," as he called it (line 18), was not for him and happily gave up the political career that might have made him the first Roman senator ever to come from Sulmo.

Ovid began to read his poems in public (a custom just coming into existence at that time) when his "beard had been cut once or twice" (*Tr.* 4.10.57–58)—in other words, perhaps around age seventeen or eighteen, in 26 or 25 B.C. Though by this time two of the great poets of the first century B.C., Lucretius (94–55?) and Catullus (85–55?), were dead, poetry still thrived in the capital. Vergil (70–19) had written the *Eclogues* and *Georgics* and was working on the *Aeneid;* Horace (65–8) had published his Satires and his Epodes and was at work on the Odes; Propertius (50 B.C.?–A.D. 2?) and Tibullus (55?–19 B.C.) were writing love elegies. Augustus favored the arts as a part of his attempt to rebuild Rome physically and spiritually after the debilitating years of civil war. Two distinguished patrons of the arts, Maecenas and Messalla, encouraged poets and supported those who needed financial help. It was, in fact, a time more favorable to enterprise in poetry than in politics, for, though all the old offices of the Roman republic remained, most of the power was in the hands of Augustus. It was dangerous to be politically ambitious, and politicians who became too powerful were likely to be short-lived. Cornelius Gallus, for instance, poet, statesman, and friend of Vergil, was forced to commit suicide in 27 or 26 B.C., apparently because he seemed dangerously intent on increasing his own prestige in Egypt. A good time, thus, for poets who stayed out of politics; and for a *young* poet, as Ovid then was, it must have been intoxicating.

The Amores

Ovid's first published work was probably the *Amores* or *Loves*. The title is difficult to translate. *Amor*, in the singular, means "love" or "Cupid," god of love. In the plural *amores* can also refer to girlfriends, love affairs, or love poems. The poems were originally published in five books; the edition we have is a second edition of three books "so that even if you get no pleasure from reading us, the pain will be less, since two books have been taken away." We do not know the publication dates of either edition, but we do know that the first came out early in Ovid's career and the second in all probability after he had already written the *Heroides* and the *Ars Amatoria*. Both are mentioned specifically in *Amores* 2.18, if the reference to *artes teneri Amoris* (the arts of tender love, 2.18.9) refers, as I think, to the *Ars* and not to the *Amores*. He may also have written his play the *Medea* by that time, if the reference to tragedy in that poem (13–14) is to be taken literally (and if indeed *Amores* 2.18 belongs to the second edition; I think it does, but we have no way of being sure).

The *Amores* are short poems between 18 and 106 lines in length, written in the first person in elegiac couplets, which proved to be Ovid's favorite meter and which he used in all his poems except the *Metamorphoses* and his lost tragedy, *Medea*. (For the meter, see the Metrical Appendix.) We will find Ovid later experimenting with the elegiac couplet to make it do things no one had done with it in Latin before; in this early stage of his poetic career he chose precisely the meter that a Roman reader would have expected for the type of poem he

was writing, although he handled it in new ways, as we will
see in chapter 3.

Roman poetry is always as much about literature as it is
about life. Because this is so, many of us were taught to think
of the Romans as second-rate imitators of the glory that was
Greece. Actually the Romans were not slavish imitators; they
were creative adaptors. Every Latin poem I can think of prof-
its from being read against its literary background, both
Greek and Roman. Ovid's earliest poems were written in the
tradition of what is generally called "love elegy," developed
in Latin by Gallus (the poet mentioned above, whose work is
lost except for a handful of surprisingly unimpressive frag-
ments), Tibullus, and Propertius, all listed by Ovid as his
forerunners (*Tristia* 4.10.51–54). We can tell almost nothing
about love elegy from the fragments of Gallus. The sixteen
poems of Tibullus and the ninety-odd poems of Propertius
define the genre as we know it before Ovid, and Ovid makes
it clear in *Amores* 1.1 that Propertius is his chief literary an-
tecedent.

In the earlier elegiac tradition the speaker is hopelessly,
passionately in love. He writes love poems because he has no
choice—he is so overwhelmed by his love that he cannot write
in a more serious and nobler vein. The poet-lover's choice of
the elegiac couplet as his meter confirms this claim, for it was
used on the whole for fairly light subjects, whereas its cousin,
the dactylic hexameter, was used for weightier matters, in-
cluding didactic poetry (Lucretius and Vergil), and epic, the
"queen of poetry" (Ennius and Vergil). The poet-lover is as
little capable of following a proper Roman career (in the army
or the law courts or politics) as he is of writing a proper Ro-
man type of poetry—Roman in the sense Cleopatra meant
when she said of Antony:

He was disposed to mirth; but on the sudden
A Roman thought hath struck him.
                                        [Shakespeare, *Antony and Cleopatra* 1.2]

The situation I have described is the basic elegiac situation, the setting for the elegiac poet's thoughts on love and life, poetry and politics, the individual and the state. The resulting poems are surprisingly varied for so limited a setting and manage to say quite a lot for all their apparent simplicity and proclaimed humbleness of form.

Ovid's poet-lover, like his predecessors', claims to be desperately in love, but he does so in such a way that we do not believe him; he too claims to be forced to write love elegy rather than epic—his opening poem actually shows his metamorphosis from epic to elegiac poet—but we know that he is playing with us. Ovid emphasizes what was present but much less prominent in earlier elegy: its capacity for comedy and satire.

Most of the fifty poems that make up the volume of *Amores* are devoted to the subjects of poetry and love. They take up nearly every conceivable mood and situation connected with being in love and writing poems about it. Ovid even includes two poems on abortion (2.13 and 14) and one on impotence (3.7) in the collection. Many of the topics, but not the last two, are standard, as is the language used to describe them: the lover as a soldier in the campaigns of love, as an *exclusus amator*, or "shut-out lover," and so on. Ovid's originality is evident neither in the subject matter, on the whole, nor in his language—it lies in his shattering the conventions of the genre so that no one could write elegy in the style of Tibullus and Propertius again.

The Heroides

At about the same time that he was completing the *Amores*, perhaps, Ovid wrote the *Heroides* or *Heroines*, a collection of fifteen verse letters addressed by women to the men they love. Each of the women but one is a character from myth; each letter expresses the feelings of the woman at a moment of great crisis in her life. Among them are letters from Penelope to Ulysses after nearly twenty years of waiting for her husband's return; from Briseis to Achilles, after she has been taken from him and given to Agamemnon in exchange for Chryseis; from Phaedra to her stepson, Hippolytus, declaring her love for him; from Dido to Aeneas after he has sailed off in search of Italy; from Hermione (married against her will to Achilles' son, Neoptolemus) to Orestes, to whom she had been betrothed; from Ariadne to Theseus, who deserted her after she helped him kill the Minotaur; from Medea to Jason after he had deserted her for Creusa; and, finally, from the one "historical" heroine, the seventh-century Greek poet Sappho to her lover Phaon. (Some scholars think that *Heroides* 15 is not by Ovid. It is not included in all the manuscripts, but it seems to have been regarded as Ovidian at an early date, and I think Ovid probably wrote it.) The version of the *Heroides* that has reached us also contains three paired letters: Paris to Helen, Leander to Hero, and Acontius to Cydippe, with each lady's response. They were probably written and published later in Ovid's career, after a poet friend of his named Sabinus had pointed the way by writing poetic answers to some of the single *Heroides* (*Epistulae ex Ponto* 4.16.13–16; *Amores* 2.18.27–34).

The *Heroides* are much more original than the *Amores*, because Ovid is breaking new ground, not working in an established tradition. Euripides had pointed the way, of course, in his tragedies about Hecuba and Phaedra and Medea and other passion-filled females. Sulpicia (the only female Roman poet whose work—just six poems—has come down to us) had addressed brief poetic letters to her lover Cerinthus at some period early in the Augustan Age. And Propertius had introduced the long poetic letter from a woman to a man into Roman elegy (4.3). It was Ovid's innovation to create a whole collection of elegiac letters, and on a single theme at

that: a woman who has lost her man. To write them Ovid had
first to think his way into the minds of the several women in
their several predicaments and then to present his analysis of
the workings of each heroine's mind, not as analysis but in
the form of dramatic monologue in her own words. Thus he
faced one of the problems Euripides faced—how to create
character through speech—but he had to do it without any
action on stage and without any other characters with whom
the heroine might interact. It was the sort of challenge Ovid
relished. As the brief descriptions above show, the plights of
the various heroines are similar: some readers have, in fact,
complained of monotony. Actually, however, Ovid's achieve-
ment must be seen as all the more spectacular for having
created within emotional situations so similar fifteen psycho-
logically plausible personalities so different from each other.

He has, moreover, boldly reinterpreted large sections of
mythological history from the point of view of one character
in the traditional story, and often a peripheral one at that.
Whereas epic and tragedy portray heroes, usually male, as
the stars of their stories, in the *Heroides* Ovid lets the under-
dogs speak. Pawns in the masculine game of war, such as
Briseis. Damaged children of the great, such as Hermione and
Orestes. Women betrayed, deserted or left behind by their
hero-lovers, such as Hypsipyle, Oenone, Laodamia, and Pe-
nelope. History, or mythology, as presented by men for men,
is one thing, but what of the women who are left behind by
these "heroes." What happens to them? Ovid makes us look
behind the usual version of the tale to see what is omitted—
that is, what became of the people who just happened to be
in the hero's way. By his treatment of the women in the *He-
roides* Ovid makes us reinterpret many aspects of these lives
to which we had never given a thought.

Coming to the *Heroides* as (probably) Ovid's next major
work after at least the first version of the *Amores* we are likely

to be struck by the way they complement love elegy while adding something new. Love elegy featured a Roman and his lady—Gallus and Lycoris, Tibullus and Delia or Nemesis, Propertius and Cynthia, Ovid and Corinna. In the *Heroides* a mythological female replaces the Roman male as the lover. Ovid has thus reversed the situation of love elegy and located it in the world of Greek myth instead of Augustan Rome. But the language and concerns are similar. When Sappho says to Phaon at *Heroides* 15.96 begging him to return to her: "I don't ask you to *love* but to let yourself be loved," she sounds much like the lover of *Amores* 1.3.1–2. Thus the *Heroides* expand the boundaries of love elegy and incorporate the world of epic within the world of elegy, beginning the process of standing the Establishment's mythology on its head that reaches its culmination in the *Metamorphoses*.

Medea

Not surprisingly, given his interests, Ovid also wrote a tragedy about Medea. We have no direct information about when he wrote it, but it seems to have fallen fairly early in his career. In *Tristia* 2, his defense of his life and work, pretty certainly written in A.D. 9, he mentions the *Medea* (along with the *Fasti* and the *Metamorphoses*) as one of his serious works (547–56). *Amores* 3.1, in addition, depicts a comic contest for Ovid's talent between Tragedy and Elegy and concludes with Tragedy allowing Elegy to keep him just a little longer. This might but need not suggest that Ovid was either working on or thinking about trying his hand at a tragedy (so, perhaps, does the reference to tragedy in *Amores* 2.18). It is possible that he was inspired to write it by his work on the *Heroides;* it is equally possible that the *Medea* suggested to him that it would be interesting to turn the tragic monologue into the literary letter. In any case it was typical of Ovid to try his hand at related kinds of poetry at the same, or approximately the same, time. (We know that he worked on the *Metamorphoses* and the *Fasti*, very different kinds of narrative, simultaneously, since work on both came to a halt with his exile in A.D. 8.) The play does not survive (apart from two lines quoted by later Roman writers), although it was thought to be very successful. Quintilian (ca. A.D. 40–100), a Roman professor of literature who usually finds Ovid frivolous, wrote that the *Medea* showed what the poet was capable of when he disciplined his talent. The Roman historian Tacitus (ca. A.D. 55–after 115) called Ovid's play one of the greatest Roman tragedies—high praise for a poet who had never written a tragedy before. It is curious that Ovid never wrote another. Perhaps the reason he did not was his desire ever to move on to new territory and new challenges. What can Ovid's *Medea* have been like? It is hard to imagine what Ovid could have found to do with the subject that had not been done before either by his Greek predecessors or by himself (if the *Heroides* are earlier than the *Medea*). We can be fairly sure that it differed from any existing version. The difficulty of creating something new out of a famous myth may well have been the challenge. Perhaps Ovid never wrote another tragedy because he felt he had failed. One can imagine that what Quintilian liked because it fit his ideas of poetic decorum might not have satisfied Ovid.

Didactic Poems

Whatever his reason for abandoning tragedy, Ovid had more to say on the subject of love. I imagine him asking himself what he could do with the subject that no one had attempted in elegiac verse before and, being Ovid, coming up with an answer at once perfectly natural, considering the nature of previous love elegy, and at the same time absolutely new and delightfully outrageous. Latin love elegy had always had a strong didactic strain, and Ovid had exploited this attribute in his own ironical way. Often characters within his earlier poems instruct other characters, as when the bawd Dipsas lectures Corinna on the art of taking a lover for all he's worth (*Am.* 1.8), or when the poet-lover gives his girlfriend a short course in silent communication before the banquet they will attend, she with her husband, he jealously looking on (*Am.* 1.4). He even presumes to advise the husband, tongue in cheek, about how best to protect her from such rakes as himself (*Am.* 3.4). He also lectures the doorman (*Am.* 1.6) and the maid (*Am.* 1.11). Thus it is not surprising that Ovid hit on the brilliant, and, as far as we know, absolutely original, idea of writing didactic poetry on the art of seduction. He wrote three poems in this field: *Medicamina Faciei,* or *On Cosmetics,* a short poem, of which we have only one hundred lines; his didactic masterpiece, the *Ars Amatoria,* or *Art of Love;* and his postscript to the didactic collection, the *Remedia Amoris,* or *Remedies for Love.*

Medicamina Faciei   The *Medicamina* was probably the first poem in this vein that Ovid wrote, a dry run, perhaps, for the more elaborate poems to follow. Its declared purpose is to instruct young ladies in the arts of beauty in order that they may be attractive to men. A long introduction sets out the importance of the subject matter the professor intends to impart. He argues that beauty must be tended and "cultivated," just as crops must be, thus suggesting that his work belongs to the same category of poetry as Vergil's *Georgics*. As the *Georgics* teaches the need for hard work as a moral virtue to wring a living out of the land, the *Medicamina* teaches the cultivation of physical beauty to please men. So much for the Roman work ethic! The professor continues his lecture with recipes for skin care. The whole thing is made funny by the

sustained incongruity between the seeming seriousness of the
instructor's attitude and the triviality of the subject. He is
clearly an expert in his field—he gives us weights and mea-
sures of the different ingredients for facial packs, much as
Vergil gives the specifics of the farmer's trade, although one
could no more make face cream from Ovid's directions than
one could build a plow from Vergil's. But it certainly *sounds*
good, well researched and suitably technical. The elegance of
the style matches the elegance of the ladies who use these
beauty aids. Many of the ingredients—eggs, honey, barley,
seeds, and beans—are, of course, staples of the agricultural
world Ovid is playing with in this delightful fragment of di-
dactic. (And they are apparently more or less the same ingre-
dients as cosmetologists today use for facials.)

Ars Amatoria   The *Ars Amatoria* is a poem in three books,
the first two probably finished by 2 or 1 B.C., the third by
A.D. 2, at the same time as the *Remedia*. In the *Ars* Ovid takes
up the challenge implicit in his own and in earlier love elegy,
that the poet-lover can teach a course in love based on his
own (literary) experiences. He writes what purports to be a
scholarly treatise following in the footsteps of Vergil and also
of Lucretius, who had written the *De Rerum Natura*, or *On the
Nature of Things*, a serious philosophical poem in which he
described the workings of the universe and man's role in it
in impassioned verse. Ovid pretends to equal seriousness.
His poem is a handbook full of technical knowledge to inform
us of all we need to know in order to pursue . . . not the good
life, but love, and not love as Plato would define it, but love
as the art of seduction.

The poem seems to have been planned in two books
addressed to men. The speaker gives a synopsis of his theme
(1.35–40) as a lecture on three subjects: (1) the best hunting
grounds in Rome to look for girls (among them porticoes,

theaters, and the Circus Maximus during horse races); (2) hunting techniques (using her servants to advance your suit, flattering letters, promises, tears, and so on); (3) the art of keeping the girl once she's been caught (constant vigilance, hard work, and attention to appearances). These are, in outline, the subjects of the first two books of the poem; hunting grounds take up lines 41–262 of Book 1, lines 263 to the end of the book are devoted to methods of capture, and Book 2 is given over to the art of holding on to the prey: "By my art she's been caught, by my art she must be held" (2.12). The book ends with success:

> I have armed you. Vulcan armed Achilles—conquer with the gifts you have been given, as he did. But whoever overcomes the Amazon by my sword, let him inscribe on his spoils, "Naso was my teacher."
>
> [2.741–44]

One couplet remains, however:

> Look—delicate girls ask me to give them instruction, you will be the next concern of my pages.
>
> [745–46]

Clearly Ovid added this later when he had decided to write a third book instructing women in the arts of love:

> I have armed the Greeks against the Amazons. There are weapons left, Penthesilea [the legendary Amazon queen] that I must give to you and your troops. Go to battle as equals; let those conquer whom gentle Venus favors, and the boy who flies throughout the world.
>
> [3.1–4]

Most of the advice in Book 3 has to do with appearance and behavior: how to overcome the faults of nature in order to attract men. Pay attention to makeup (and never let a man see you without it), but don't overdo; make the best of your attributes—don't laugh if your teeth are bad, and be sure to choose a position for lovemaking that shows off your charms and conceals your weak points. The *Ars* is more ambitious than the *Amores* and even than the *Heroides*. For one thing it is much longer than anything Ovid had written before—even before it received its third book it contained 1,518 lines, to which Book 3 contributed an additional 812. More important than length, it is also *one* poem, not a collection of poems, and has to sustain one voice over its length. It also attempts more than the *Amores*. In the *Ars* Ovid takes on and parodies love elegy and didactic while poking fun along the way at the political and moral climate of Augustan Rome. There is, perhaps, little in the *Ars* for which the careful reader of the *Amores* would not be prepared, but the parody, burlesque, and social commentary were probably more noticeable in the sustained voice of didactic than they were in the fragmented voices of lowly elegy, and thus it was the *Ars* that got Ovid into trouble. But this is moving ahead of ourselves. At the time of its publication the *Ars* does not seem to have caused its author any problems. He went on to write the *Remedia* and then the *Metamorphoses* and the *Fasti* before there were any repercussions.

The Remedia   At about the time he was writing the third book of the *Ars*, Ovid hit on the wonderful idea of writing a sequel in which love's victims would learn how to escape their predicament. His professor-speaker in the poem begins by attempting to convince Cupid that this new approach is not a betrayal of love, because it is only addressed to those who are unhappy, and then goes on to demonstrate its importance. All of mythological history would have been different, it seems, if the narrator had been around to teach the art of falling out of love: Dido would be alive, Tereus wouldn't have raped Philomela, Pasiphae wouldn't have copulated with the bull, and Phaedra would have known how to resist the charms of her stepson, Hippolytus. Indeed, there would have been no Trojan War, and so, presumably, no *Iliad*, no *Odyssey*, and no *Aeneid* (not to mention the *Heroides*). The implications of the professor's boast are comically catastrophic, for much of world literature would never have been written, had Doctor Ovid been in residence at the right time.

Most of the poem is devoted to descriptions of some forty cures for love, as Ovid neatly reverses most of the advice he gave in the *Ars*: Make your girl do whatever shows off her flaws—have her dance, if she can't dance, and sing if she has no voice. Be sure to get in to see her in the morning before she has her clothes and her face on (331ff.). The speaker even, for once, joins forces with moralists and philosophers in condemning idleness and sloth. Take up politics, law, or a military career, he says, all of these traditionally anathema to the elegiac lover. Above all, stop reading love poetry—avoid Ovid, Callimachus, Philetas, Sappho, Anacreon, Tibullus, Propertius, and Gallus (757ff.)!

The Metamorphoses

With the *Remedia* Ovid finished his career as a love poet in the strict sense, although he would return to the topic of love frequently in future poems. He was now over forty, very popular, and looking for still greater challenges. The ultimate challenge was, of course, epic. And the grand master of epic was, of course, Vergil, who had created a national epic for Rome during Ovid's first years in the capital. But now Vergil had been dead for twenty years, and Ovid set out to challenge him on his own ground. He worked on his great mythological poem, his only work in dactylic hexameter, the meter of epic, until A.D. 8, when he was banished. The poem was published without the poet's final revisions (just as the *Aeneid* was, for different reasons), but it is complete as it is in fifteen books. Ovid might well have polished it up here and there, but there is no reason to suppose that he would have made major changes. The *Metamorphoses* is Ovid's answer to Vergil, but it is far more than that. It is unique in Classical poetry in that it is simultaneously an answer to so many earlier poets in the most diverse genres—to Homer and to Apollonius of Rhodes (the third-century author of the *Argonautica*), to the Greek tragedians, and to Callimachus (the third-century author of the *Aetia*, a long episodic poem, and of numerous hymns and epigrams, a Greek poet who had a vast influence on the poets of Ovid's day and earlier). (For details, see my remarks on the *Fasti* below and chap. 4.) The *Metamorphoses* is perhaps Ovid's most innovative work, an epic on a majestic scale that refuses to take epic seriously. It is also Ovid's greatest and, to my mind, most delightful poem. If I were to be marooned on that desert island to which, in the fantasies of childhood, we were always allowed to take only three books, the *Metamorphoses* would be one of my choices. In fifteen books Ovid whisks us magically from the creation of the world out of chaos through Europe, Asia, and Africa over centuries of mythological time to Augustan Rome. Along the way he tells some 250 stories from Greek mythology, Roman legend, and Roman history, linked into one continuous account by means of a vaguely chronological frame. Many of the characters that most of us have known from childhood, often unaware of their source, are from the *Metamorphoses*: the teenage Phaëthon who cannot control the horses of his father, the Sun; Baucis and Philemon, the devoted old couple who receive the gods into their humble home and are rewarded for their piety; the giant Polyphemus, who (unlike his counterpart in the *Odyssey*) combs his hair with a rake because he is madly in love

with Galatea, who is madly in love with Acis; Venus in love
with the young Adonis, who *will* go boar hunting despite her
warnings; the artist Daedalus, whose son, Icarus, flies too
close to the sun; Narcissus in love with his own image; Pyg-
malion in love with the statue he has made; Arachne the
weaver turned into a spider—all these and many more are so
vividly depicted by Ovid that even where other Classical ver-
sions of the stories exist, it is likely to be Ovid's that we
remember. In many cases only Ovid's survives, while most
of the works on which he drew are lost to us.

Ovid is a masterful storyteller with an eye for the kind
of detail that brings people alive and creates scenes never to
be forgotten. The virgin Callisto, one of the nymphs of Diana's
chaste band, taken in by Jupiter's disguise as Diana and so
caught alone and raped by him in a grove, "almost forgot to
take her quiver and her arrows and the bow she had hung
up" when she fled afterwards (*Meta.* 2.439–40). How fitting
this comment is, both psychologically and symbolically. All
she wants to do is get away from the horrible place, we feel;
and, of course, she has no right to the weapons of virginity
any longer, as will be brought home when Diana, discovering
her pregnancy, expels her from her band. Later in the book,
when Mercury, flying over Athens, catches sight of Herse and
falls in love, what does the god do before he goes to meet
her?:

> He doesn't disguise himself, so confident is he in his
> looks; as is reasonable, though, he helps them by taking
> some trouble, combs his hair and arranges his cloak to
> fall nicely.
>
> [*Meta.* 2.731–34]

Just like the modern teenager who whips the brush out of his
back pocket, Mercury makes sure he is looking his best. A

wonderful detail to set the scene for a love affair between an
attractive young god and a pretty young girl. Ovid had shown a flair for narrative from the beginning.
Here for the first time he could let it loose in a medium where
stories *are* the poem and not just illustrations or digressions.
Fragments of myth had been included in elegy at least since
Propertius. (We cannot tell what Gallus did; on the whole
Tibullus avoided using myth in his poems.) Ovid made myth
his subject in the *Heroides*, but his verse form, the poetic letter,
limited what he could do with it. With the *Metamorphoses* there
were no limits to what he could do with narrative and with
myth, and he did it all. His stories range from a few to
hundreds of lines; some he tells in elaborate detail, some so
obscurely that you will not know what he is talking about
unless you happen to know the story already (or look it up
in a Classical dictionary). Some are comedies; some are trag-
edies (or as close to tragedy as Ovid ever gets); some he tells
from changing points of view, often seemingly engaged with
his characters, at other times distant from or even mocking
them; still other stories he entrusts to subnarrators who have
their own points of view; the *Metamorphoses* also contains sto-
ries within stories: when Ovid tells of Orpheus, who tells of
Venus telling Adonis the tale of Atalanta and Meleager
(Book 10), we are hearing a story within a story within a story
within a story. Never before had Greek myth been presented
like this.

The Fasti

At the same time that Ovid was working on the *Meta-
morphoses* he was writing the *Fasti*. The *Fasti* is a long poem
in elegiac couplets based on the Roman calendar (called *fasti*
in Latin). The six books that he completed go through the first
six months of the year describing religious rituals, explaining

their origins, and giving astronomical information about the
rising and setting of the constellations. Overall, the *Fasti* is
probably the least appealing of Ovid's poems to a modern
reader, although it is filled with fascinating bits of arcane in-
formation and contains a few of his best stories. It seems
never to have been finished. Perhaps Ovid became bored by
it. Except for a few insertions in Book 1, it exists more or less
as he must have left it in A.D. 8 at the time of his exile. It was
certainly the most intransigent poetic form he ever chose. The
organization by days and months resulted in fragmentation,
and the two main themes—celestial phenomena and religious
ritual—do not seem, to a modern reader at any rate, to have
much connection. Though the poem has wonderful moments,
reading it is like a trek through a desert to reach an oasis.

It is hard to know just how to take the *Fasti*. The only
thing I am certain of is that it was intended to take up what
Propertius promised in the opening of his fourth book and
then backed off from. At the midpoint of the first poem of
Book 4, Propertius says,

> I shall sing of rites and days and the early names of
> places; this is the goal my horse should sweat toward,
>
> [4.1.69–70]

announcing the kind of program that the Greek poet Calli-
machus would have approved. Callimachus, who influenced
every extant Roman poet from Catullus to Ovid, advocated
writing short, carefully wrought poems or longer poems made
up, like Hesiod's, or like his own *Aetia*, or *Causes*, of short
units strung together rather than continuous mythological
epic, which by the third century B.C., when he was writing,
seemed to him outmoded (even though his own contempo-
rary, Apollonius of Rhodes, continued to write it). Nearly all
late-Republican and Augustan poets claim allegiance to Cal-
limachean poetics. One form this claim takes is adherence to

Hesiod (rather than to Homer), as Propertius here suggests with his reference to rites and days. When a Roman poet announces that he is following Hesiod, he is generally claiming that he is writing in the tradition of Callimachus. Propertius had specifically claimed allegiance to Callimachus in the opening words of Book 3, and here, in the opening poem of Book 4, just before the lines quoted above, he called himself the "Roman Callimachus" (4.1.64). The lines come just before a figure named Horos appears and, in a long-winded speech, tells the poet to go on with love elegy instead of turning to aetiological poetry:

> But you should shape elegies, tricky work—this is your camp ground—so the rest of the crowd will write following your example.
>
> [135–36]

The rest of Book 4 shows this divided intention: poems 2, 4, 9, and 10 are aetiological poems explaining the origins of Roman cults and customs by relating them to distant people and events, 3, 6, and 11 deal in some fashion with Augustan topics, and the remaining three are connected with elegiac love (7 and 8 about Propertius's lover Cynthia, 5 about a *lena*, or bawd). The best poems by far are the Cynthia poems. Ovid probably decided that Propertius's aborted program was worth following up and that by carrying it out he would outdo Propertius (as he may well have felt he had already done with his *Amores*) and create something new in elegiac verse. Even if Propertius had limited his fourth book to poems about days and rituals, it would still have been a collection of snippets, not a single Roman poem. At the same time, by outdoing Propertius when he was playing the Roman Callimachus, Ovid would make clear who the Roman Callimachus really was. So far I feel fairly sure I know what Ovid is up to.

What I cannot decide, however, is whether the *Fasti*,

being, as E. J. Kenney says, "*res Romana* served up à la grecque," is therefore essentially frivolous, as he thinks (Cambridge History of Latin: *Age of Augustus*, p. 134). It is certainly true that there is a discrepancy between manner and matter, but the poem may be serious in its own way. At the least I think that it is a serious attempt to show that the elegiac couplet (which is usually thought inadequate to narrative because it moves in two-line blocks that turn in on themselves and so are closed in a way that hexameters are not) can be made to work well to tell a story. When we compare Ovid's treatment of the story of Ceres and the rape of Persephone in the *Fasti* with his version in the *Metamorphoses* we can see how carefully he tailored each to its medium. Since he was working on his epic of sorts (the *Metamorphoses*) and his Hesiodic-Callimachean-Propertian aetiological poem (the *Fasti*) at the same time, showing, as Wilkinson says, "his nonchalant versatility by espousing at one and the same time both sides in the Alexandrian and Neoteric Battle of the Books" ("The World of the '*Metamorphoses*'," *Ovidiana* [1958]), would it not be like him to refuse to take the Roman and Heroic seriously in his epic, which is supposed to be the loftier genre, while using the less heroic elegiac verse for his more Roman poem? I think it likely, but my readers must see what they think.

What is most interesting to me about the *Fasti* is its series of narrators. The main narrator is "Ovid," who seems to be an amiable but not very bright student investigating the origins of Roman religious festivals, a slippery topic, it turns out, because there are as many opinions as there are authorities. The student does his best; he asks the divinities themselves to explain what is what. Sometimes he gets answers— as when Janus, the two-headed god of doorways and of January, explains why he has two heads (so he can look both ways without having to waste time by turning his neck) and why the offerings to him are dates and honey (so that sweetness may last through the new year). At another time he is given three conflicting answers, each by the goddess who claims that June is named after her: Juno from her name, Hebe from her title as goddess of young people (that is, *juniors*), and Concordia because of her role in joining (*junctis*) Sabines and Romans after the rape of the Sabine women. Faced with such conflicting testimony, the speaker, remembering the result of the judgment of Paris, refuses to commit himself to any of the derivations claimed. As John Fyler has said, "the narrator's emphasis on his attention to verifiable fact, in the midst of explanatory chaos, becomes a recurrent comic device" (*Chaucer and Ovid* [New Haven, 1979], p. 14).

One of my favorite tales in the *Fasti* concerns the origin of the festival of Anna Perenna, an ancient Italian divinity whose rustic festival in March involved a great deal of drinking by the banks of the Tiber and people staggering home drunk to the amusement of the crowd. Since by Ovid's day no one knew who Anna Perenna really was, he offers an apparent explanation launching, with no warning, into epic parody:

> Poor Dido had already burned—once in the flame of love for Aeneas, and afterwards in the funeral bonfire she had built for herself.
>
> [*F.* 3.545–46]

In this slightly patronizing way Ovid picks up where Book 4 of the *Aeneid* left off. After Dido's suicide, says Ovid, piecing out Vergil's story with episodes of which Vergil never dreamed, the neighboring Africans capture the palace, forcing her sister Anna to flee. After being refused sanctuary by the king of Malta because of his fear of her brother Pygmalion, who, as readers of the *Aeneid* will remember, killed Dido's husband, Sychaeus, Anna sails for southern Italy—no further off, the poet assures us with epic solemnity, than nine times the distance of a slingshot (583–84). It is a fair guess that this delightfully specific measurement of distance would not have told a Roman of Ovid's day much more than it tells us, which is absolutely nothing, but it has at least the requisite mock-epic ring. Our narrator is not going to spare us such touches. An epic journey needs also an epic sea storm, and, of course, he provides one. It is only a little storm in comparison with its famous fellow in *Aeneid* 1, but, after all, this is only a little voyage—nine "slingshot" lengths, in fact. Ovid clearly wants us to associate this journey with Aeneas's, because he characterizes Anna with words frequently used by Vergil about Aeneas: "refugee" and "storm-tossed." Furthermore, when a gust of wind suddenly blows Anna to shore, who should be waiting there but Achates—in the *Aeneid*, Aeneas's silent but faithful friend? For in fact she has been blown in to Lavinium, Aeneas's home after the events of the *Aeneid*. Aeneas hospitably takes her home with him, but Lavinia, his wife, is not pleased. Insanely jealous, she plots murder. Anna is warned in a vision (as Aeneas was warned against Dido by Mercury) and escapes, like a deer terrified by the sound of wolves (epic simile). The narrator is not quite sure what happened to her next but seems to think that she was concealed by the river god Numicus and so is called Anna Perenna from the Latin words for perennial river (*amnis perennus*).

But now, suddenly, having given this explanation of the name at much greater length than I have, our narrator hastily offers four other explanations for the name (657–60). To these he adds yet another story, assuring us that this one is "not far from the truth." In this version Anna was an old woman who distributed food to Roman citizens during a famine in 494 B.C. and was rewarded for her kindness by a statue set up in her honor. Somehow she then became a goddess at whose festivals obscenities were sung by young girls, behind which curious custom is a story Ovid relates with some relish:

Mars asked for Anna's help in his pursuit of Minerva; Anna, pretending that Minerva was interested, disguised herself as Minerva and entered Mars's bedroom. Mars attempted to kiss the goddess before realizing his mistake. Anna laughed at him, Venus was delighted, and ever since young girls have sung ribald songs and told jokes in memory of Anna's duping of Mars (677ff.). The "epic" sequel to the *Aeneid* is presented as the true explanation of Anna Perenna, only to be undercut by four totally different explanations immediately followed by another story as unlikely as the first, which our narrator gravely assures us is probably true. Here, as elsewhere, a reader finds his leg being pulled. (We will see Ovid doing much more elaborately in the *Metamorphoses* what he does here.)

The Poems from Exile

In A.D. 8, when the *Metamorphoses* was so nearly finished that copies were circulating among Ovid's friends and six books of the *Fasti* existed in a fairly complete draft, Ovid was banished from Rome by the emperor Augustus and his books were removed from the public libraries. His place of exile was to be Tomis, a colony founded by Greeks in the seventh century B.C. on the site of modern Constanza in Romania—in Ovid's day, apparently, inhabited for the most part by Getans, a Thracian tribe. It was a barren, uncivilized place where Ovid never felt safe from attack. The winters were so cold, he claims, that one's hair froze into icicles, and wine had to be chopped into servings. Indeed, the mighty Danube froze so hard that wagons could be pulled along it (*Tr.* 3.10). And to make the scene even more unendurable, no one spoke Latin, few spoke Greek. Ovid doubtless exaggerates the conditions there for rhetorical effect, but it must have been a grim place for a Roman city-dweller to find himself in. Yet in spite of many ardent petitions from the poet and his many friends in Rome, Augustus did not relent; he never allowed Ovid to move to a more civilized place of exile or to return to Italy. Nor did the emperor Tiberius, who succeeded Augustus in A.D. 14, recall him. Ovid died in exile in late A.D. 17 or early 18, never having seen his beloved Rome again.

Why was Ovid banished? We do not know, but we can venture an informed guess. Consider for a moment what was happening in Augustan Rome during the years Ovid was writing the poems we have looked at. In A.D. 8, Augustus had been in control for nearly forty years and had worked hard to give Rome a new image. Rome was now a large, cosmopolitan city with luxuries flowing in from all over the empire. Morals were fairly lax, divorce was easy to arrange, adultery was common, and the family seemed to have lost much of its coherence—the same situation some think they see around them today. Augustus wanted to turn back the clock and restore such old Republican virtues as chastity, poverty, fidelity, sobriety, and piety. Rome's legends as found in the early books of the historian Livy give us the atmosphere— the matron Lucretia, raped by the wicked Tarquin, commits suicide lest she be an example of unchastity (albeit unwilling) to Roman womanhood; Horatius heroically chops down the bridge to keep the enemy at bay; the general Regulus, captured by the Carthaginians and sent to negotiate terms, forbids the Romans to negotiate and returns to Carthage to be tortured; Mucius Scaevola thrusts his hand proudly in the flames to show the quality of Roman courage, and so on. Such had been the imagined heroes of Rome at its greatest, and Augustus wanted to recapture the spirit of those days. In addition, one could add, he pragmatically wanted to jack up the sagging birth rate of the upper classes and rekindle a sense of national duty to encourage the young to serve the state. Accordingly, Augustus tried to legislate morality. In

28 b.c.(?), in 18 b.c., and in a.d. 9 he passed legislation designed to promote marriage and procreation and to make adultery a capital crime. Augustus's own morals do not seem to have been all they might have been, even if we discount most of the gossip about his taste for young boys and young virgins. Certainly his divorce of Scribonia immediately after she gave birth to a daughter did nothing to promote the ideal of the sanctity of marriage. And what of his marrying Livia when she was six months pregnant or his forcing first Agrippa and then Tiberius to divorce a beloved wife in order to marry his daughter, Julia? A discrepancy between public statements and private actions must have been obvious to all with eyes to see.

There was a further discrepancy between the emperor's proclaimed desire to return to the simplicity and values of the old days and his desire to make a splendid showpiece of Rome. He is said to have forced his womenfolk to spin and weave their own cloth as an example to all of the virtues of simplicity and hard work. At the same time he proudly proclaimed that he found Rome brick and left it marble. It is true that many of the new and restored buildings were temples and might, therefore, be justified by his policy of reviving the old reverence for the gods. But others were places of entertainment, and even the temples were much more elaborate than piety alone dictated. As Ovid has the god Janus say in the *Fasti*,

> we too like golden temples, even though we *approve* of old-fashioned ones
>
> [1.223–24]

and

> we *praise* the olden days, we *enjoy* our own.
>
> [1.225]

There was much matter for a satirist in Augustan Rome, and Ovid was a satirist of sorts who had a disconcerting habit of seeing too clearly and commenting on what he saw. One of the things that is likely to be most attractive to us in Ovid is his blithe refusal to toe the party line. Right up to the time he was exiled and even, sporadically, afterwards, he refused to take seriously the things that Augustus was trying to promote. He did not attack the emperor or his spokesmen; he either eloquently ignored all that Augustus was promoting or subverted it by showing its hypocrisy or its impracticality. Augustus was offended by the *Ars*, Ovid tells us again and again, and in the next chapter we shall see why. But there was also much in Ovid's other works to annoy Rome's "first citizen," as he liked to be called. Phaedra, for example, trying to persuade her stepson, Hippolytus, in *Heroides* 4 that there is nothing wrong with a stepmother going to bed with her stepson, claims that old-fashioned piety like his went out with the Golden Age, which was, moreover, a very uncouth and boorish epoch. The Golden Age, however, was an important Augustan theme. It incorporated an essentially nostalgic vision of a long-gone ideal time when the world was young, justice reigned, and peace flourished. For some, the Peace of Augustus was a recreation of this Golden Age, which means that the emperor cannot have been very happy with the implications of Phaedra's speech. Elsewhere Ovid is still more subversive. He claims that the present age is, in fact, golden— because everything has its price, even love (*Ars* 2.277–78). Rome is golden in the sense that she is filled with the gold of her conquests (*Ars* 3.113–14). As usual, he is right. Augustus had adorned Rome to make her a showplace, and the very riches he brought in from the empire to accomplish this encouraged and enhanced the corruption and soft living that he publicly deplored. It is easy to see that Ovid must have always been a thorn in Augustus's side.

Still, something particular must have happened in A.D. 8 to cause Ovid's banishment. He claims in the *Tristia* (2.207) that a poem (according to most but not all scholars, the *Ars Amatoria*) and a "mistake" were responsible. But since the *Ars* had been published long before, it must have been the "mistake" that made Augustus decide to expel Ovid as far from Rome as he could get him. Ovid is never explicit about the error, but he insists again and again (in *Tr.* 1.2.97–100 and 4.10.89–90, for example) that it was a mistake, not a crime, something stupid but not vicious, and implies that he saw something it was dangerous to have seen. Ovid's banishment came in the same year as the banishment of Augustus's adulterous granddaughter Julia and her lover, and this came only ten years after his daughter, also named Julia, and four of her lovers were banished, a fifth being executed. All in all, Augustus must have been tired of those who seemed to mock his attempts to improve Roman morals—his family by its behavior, Ovid by his poetry. Possibly Ovid had some knowledge of a scandal concerning Julia the younger that infuriated Augustus when it came out, or perhaps he had information about some political intrigue in Augustus's family. Even if we discount much of what Suetonius relates in his *Lives of the Caesars* as unreliable gossip, it is clear that, from early days, Augustus intended to mark out a political heir to succeed him at his death and that a lot of scheming on his part and others' preceded his final choice of Tiberius as successor.

Whatever the reason, Ovid spent the rest of his life by the Black Sea. He went on writing poetry: it was both like and unlike anything he had written before and surely unlike anything he would have written had he not been banished. The poems Ovid wrote in exile are the *Tristia*, or *Poems of Sadness*, fifty poems in five books, written between A.D. 8 and around A.D. 12; the *Ibis*, an attack on an unknown enemy, exact year of composition unknown; and the *Epistulae ex Ponto*, or *Letters from Pontus*, forty-six poetic epistles in four books, written between roughly A.D. 12 or 13 and A.D. 16. A didactic poem on, of all subjects, fishing (the *Halieutica*) is found in most modern editions of Ovid's works, including the Oxford Classical Text. Even though the poem is ascribed to Ovid in the manuscripts containing it as *Versus Ovidii de piscibus et feris* (*Ovid's Verses on Fish and Wild Animals*), and by Pliny the Elder (*Natural History* 32), who paraphrases some of it, it seems to me unlikely that Ovid was the author of the 134-line fragment that has been preserved. One example should suffice; the poet is discussing the defense instincts of various kinds of fish:

> When the squid, slow of flight, chances to have been caught beneath clear water, afraid of hands destined any moment to grab it, it stains the sea by vomiting black blood, changes course and so baffles pursuing eyes.
>
> [*Halieutica* 19–22]

It is scarcely a major work of art, whoever wrote it, and I shall not discuss it further. (Two other poems ascribed to Ovid but generally considered spurious are the *Nux*, or *Nut Tree*, and the *Consolatio ad Liviam*, a consolation to Livia on the death of her son Drusus.)

The Ibis Although we cannot date the *Ibis*, it was clearly written after Book 1 of the *Tristia* (which describes Ovid's journey into exile and thus seems to contain the first poems he wrote after he left Rome) and very likely after the *Tristia* as a whole. The *Tristia* contains several poems about false friends (1.8, 3.11, and 4.9), which might well have led Ovid to experiment on a larger scale with the subject in the *Ibis*. I shall take this strange and not very successful poem up first, out of chronological order, before turning to the far more interesting series of poems contained in the *Tristia* and the *Epistulae ex Ponto*.

The *Ibis* is an invective modeled after a poem of the same name by Callimachus. Ovid again expands the boundaries of elegiac, this time by using it "for wars, even though battles are not generally fought in this meter" (43–44) and again reminds his readers that *he*, not Propertius, is truly the Roman Callimachus. One of the subjects of the *Tristia* was the behavior of those who had betrayed the sacred obligations of friendship when Ovid fell from grace, but never before had he tried such sustained imprecation (642 lines) against someone who, as he says, kicked him when he was down (29–30). In the poem he gives neither the offense nor the name of the malefactor, but he warns the culprit that the *Ibis* is only the first and gentler phase of the attack. The next phase will be a real *ad hominem* assault that will tell all, if Ibis persists in his behavior (51ff.).

The first part of the poem is fascinating. The speaker plays priest in a sacrifice in which all the usual elements are perverted. Urging those present at the ceremony to speak words of ill omen, wear black, and weep, he orders Ibis as victim to put on the sacrificial ribbons and bare his throat to the knife, as if he were a bull or a lamb. In a majestic invocation calling all the gods to witness, he summons every disaster known to man to fall on his enemy. Even after his own death the speaker will pursue him:

> Whatever I am, I shall strive to burst forth from Stygian shores and in vengeance, thrust my cold hands in your face.
>
> [151–52]

And there will be no escape for Ibis even in his own death; he will be punished with all the most famous mythological punishments. In fact, he will suffer all the ills of all the heroes of mythology.

At this point, unhappily, about halfway through, the poem degenerates into a catalogue of obscure myths. It shows extraordinary erudition, but it becomes tiresome, as catalogues tend to do. It was suggested by A. E. Housman that Ovid's studies for the *Metamorphoses* and the *Fasti* had given him so much mythological material that he was unable to use in those poems that he used the *Ibis* as an opportunity to "discharge a great part of his load of knowledge through the channel of imprecation" (*Journal of Philology* 35 [1920]: 318). He may well be right. Yet I am sure that part of the reason for Ovid's writing the poem was, as always, the challenge of doing something new with elegiac verse. Most readers will not, I think, find the *Ibis* a very impressive poem.

The Tristia and the Epistulae ex Ponto   I have often asked myself what Ovid would have written after he completed the *Metamorphoses* and the *Fasti* if he had not been banished, but I have never found an answer. The *Tristia* and the *Epistulae* form the perfect conclusion to Ovid's poetic career. But it is, of course, most improbable that he would have invented the setting of his last works if had not been exiled to Tomis. With these poems he comes full circle. He returns to the forms of poetry he wrote in his youth but now sings them in a new key. Like the *Amores*, the *Tristia* and the *Epistulae ex Ponto* are short poems in elegiac couplets written in the first person about what the speaker claims is his own experience. He has, however, taken much of the language and many of the themes of the erotic elegies and recast them for his present needs. Key words that were used thematically in the *Amores* to describe the plight of the lovesick poet now appear with blacker implications. The "wound" of love and the pain associated with it become the wound and pain that destroy the exiled

poet; the theme of the *exclusus amator*, the lover shut out of
his mistress's house to spend the night in the cold, becomes
the theme of the banished poet, excluded from everything
that means anything to him and from the source of his in-
spiration, Rome. The playfulness of the *Amores*, which tells
us that the speaker will not really die of love, is gone, and
the issues seem, and are, more serious. But in order to read
the poems right we must remember that Ovid is creating a
poetic persona here, just as he has always done.

The new persona Ovid devised for the poems from his
exile incorporates elements from the mythological heroines of
the *Heroides* as well as elements from the *Amores*. Like the
Heroides, many of the exilic poems are poetic letters written
in despair by a speaker who is suffering and alone. Most have
a specific recipient in mind and are tailored to that person.
And, in the course of the series, Ovid creates a new mythol-
ogy in much the same way that he rewrote mythology for the
Heroides. In this new mythology he depicts himself as Ulysses
and as Aeneas, as Orestes, and sometimes as Jason; his wife
back home working for his recall is the faithful Penelope; Au-
gustus is the angry Jupiter whose thunderbolt destroys.

The poems from exile are, then, clearly about life, but
they are also about poetry. The speaker, the "I" of the poems,
is based on the speaker of the *Amores*, the language is a re-
casting of the language of love elegy, and many of the situa-
tions are literary. *Tristia* 1.3 is at once a portrait of Ovid's last
night in Rome and a re-creation in elegy of an epic theme,
the sack of a city; 1.2 is an elegiac evocation of an epic sea
storm as well as (perhaps) an actual sea storm that occurred
while Ovid was en route to the Black Sea. And finally Ovid's
wife is his real wife who stayed beyind in Rome at her hus-
band's insistence even though she wanted to join him in exile;
she is also Penelope of epic and the beloved mistress of elegy.

Ovid is still experimenting with poetic genres, even

when he has been completely uprooted. And again he shows his enormous originality. In the poems from exile he not only asks the poetic forms with which he began his career to do something they had never been asked to do before; he revives at the same time the association with death and lamentation inherent in elegy from its beginnings in early Greece. Roman poets had occasionally used elegy for lamentation. Catullus's moving poem on his brother's death (poem 101) is one example; Propertius's elegy on the death of Cornelia (4.11) is another. For the most part, however, Roman elegy had been focused on love. Now Ovid expands its boundaries by stressing the "elegiac" in it.

At the same time, of course, his equation of exile with death makes his own situation seem that much more intolerable and Augustus's refusal to relent that much harsher. Setting himself a typically Ovidian challenge, he will once again take a relatively limited subject and uncover all its facets, take a worn subject and make it new. Some readers find the collection monotonous. I find it fascinating but readily acknowledge that the poems probably do not come across well in translation. Anyone who wants to read the poems from exile should read them in Latin, if at all possible. Some are superb by any standard. Others take more effort—and many of them are worth it. Books 1, 3, 4, and 5 of the *Tristia* and the four books of the *Epistulae ex Ponto* are made up of fairly short poems in which Ovid describes the horrors of the journey into exile and then the horrors of Tomis and begs to be recalled. Many of the poems in the *Tristia* are addressed to anonymous recipients and claim that it would be dangerous to the addressee if it were known that Ovid was communicating with him. The *Epistulae ex Ponto* all have named recipients.

In both collections much is made of the miseries of exile.

We see the barren, frozen landscape that, even in spring, will
not grow trees or vines, where farmers have to go armed, and
where poisoned arrows are a constant threat, even within city
walls. To contrast with this wasteland, Ovid imagines scenes
in Rome—a Roman triumph, his wife at her tasks, the reac-
tions of his friends. Poems endlessly pleading Ovid's case
pour out of Tomis, urging friends to be loyal and to work for
his recall and castigating those who rejected him in his dis-
grace.

A subject that comes up again and again in the poems is
the poet's inability to write good poetry any longer. (A reader
of the *Ibis* might well agree with Ovid's negative assessment
of his exile poetry, but we should not take it at face value.) It
makes fine rhetoric—all Augustus has to do to get great po-
etry from Ovid again is to recall him—but it is clear that Ovid
did not believe it himself (at least some of the time). See, for
example, the beginning of the last poem of the *Tristia*:

> You yourself see, wife dearer to me than myself, how
> great a memorial I have given you in my books. Fortune
> may take much from the author, but you at least will be
> made famous by my talent. As long as I am read your
> fame will be read along with me, and you cannot alto-
> gether disappear into the mournful funeral pyre.
>
> [5.14.1–6]

The man who wrote those lines (or *Tristia* 4.10.125–30) did not
think that he was writing bad poetry read by no one except
a few good friends. Even in the last poem of the *Epistulae*,
one of the most downhearted poems in the collection (and
the *Epistulae* are, on the whole, much more pessimistic than
the *Tristia*), in a poem whose last lines are as gloomy as any-
thing Ovid ever wrote:

I have lost everything; nothing but life is left to afford me
pain and the sense of it. Where is the joy in stabbing a
dead body? There is no place on me for a new wound
[4.16.49–52]

—even here Ovid speaks of his achievement, albeit in the
past tense:

Greater fame comes after death; I too had a reputation
then, even when I was counted among the living.
[4.16.3–4]

If I may speak thus, my Muse was famous, to be read by
such great men [as the Cotta and Messalla families].
[4.16.45–46]

We should not, then, take Ovid literally when he claims that
he is forgetting his Latin (*Tr.* 3.14.45ff.).

This alleged inability to write real poetry any longer is
an aspect of one of Ovid's most fascinating themes in the
poems from exile—the metamorphosis of a Roman poet into
a Getan poet—and its corollary—the transformation of a
lonely Roman exile cut off from his neighbors into a well-loved
friend surrounded by friends. *Tristia* 1.1 introduces the sub-
ject, as it does virtually everything we will find in the re-
maining poems. The poem is addressed to the poetry book
as it sets out on its long journey to Rome, where its master
is forbidden to go. The poetry is not good, Ovid claims, be-
cause he lacks the serenity of mind required for good writing:

Poems require the seclusion and peace of the writer, *I* am
tossed by the sea, by winds and wild storms.
[41–42]

Book 3 also opens with the poet's difficulty in writing and

introduces a new stage in his degeneration. He is beginning to lose his ability to write Latin (the book is speaking to a potential Roman reader):

> If by chance anything seems to you not expressed in Latin, it was a barbarous land he wrote it in.
>
> [1.17–18]

According to the last poem in the book, he is beginning to mix Getic with his Latin:

> Words often fail me when I try to say something (I'm ashamed to confess it), and I've forgotten how to talk. I'm surrounded by Thracian and Scythian voices, and it seems to me I could write in Getic meter. Believe me, I'm afraid you're reading Pontic words mixed with Latin in my writing.
>
> [14.45–50]

(Neither of the above statements is true, of course. There is no trace of anything foreign in any of the poems.) Since Ovid's Latin has been spoiled, as he claims, he can no longer be read as a Roman poet by Romans, and since the Sarmatians do not speak Latin, they cannot read him either. He is totally isolated.

Tristia 5.10 is the culmination of this theme. Here, following a fascinating description of the dangers of life in Tomis (which sounds rather like the setting of a western, with dangerous Pontic tribes replacing the Indians of the American movie world), Ovid depicts the ultimate indignity for a civilized man:

> *They* transact their business in a language they share, *I* have to communicate by gesture; I am the barbarian here, understood by no one; and the stupid Getans laugh at Latin words.
>
> [35–38]

In *Epistulae* 1.5 Ovid imagines himself writing mainly for a Getic audience:

> Why should I polish my verse with worried care? Am I to be afraid that Getans won't approve of it?
>
> [61–62]

And in 2.5 he claims that his talent is insufficient for an important subject like a Roman triumph (25–30). In the third book of the *Epistulae*, however, Ovid's characterization of his poetry and of his relationship with his neighbors begins to change. *Epistulae* 3.2 shows the poet winning the approval of the Getans and the Sarmatians for immortalizing Cotta Maximus, the recipient of the letter, through his writing. The distance between Ovid and his neighbors imagined in *Tristia* 5.10 has begun to close. Here the poet is surrounded by a friendly crowd with whom he talks in their native language. One of them is quoted as saying:

> We too, good guest, know the name of friendship, we whom the Pontus and Danube separate from the Romans.
>
> [43–44]

Barbarian and Roman are not that different, after all: everyone values friendship, as the poem demonstrates in action by the hosts' treatment of the stranger in their midst. By *Epistulae* 4.9 Ovid and his neighbors are closer still; they want him to leave because that is what he wants; for themselves they want him to stay, and they have made their admiration and affection apparent by granting him immunity (presumably from taxes, although it is not clear exactly what Ovid means [99–102]). In 4.13 Ovid's transformation into a Getic poet writing for a Getic audience is complete. He again refers to defects in his verse that result from this transformation:

You should not wonder if my verse is flawed, written by
one who is almost a Getic poet. I am ashamed, I have
written a book in Getic—barbarian words set to our me-
ters. I gave pleasure (congratulate me), and have begun
to hold the name of poet among the uncivilized Getans.
You ask the subject? You would praise it: I wrote about
Caesar.

[17–23]

Ovid's subject, he goes on to say, was the apotheosis of Au-
gustus Caesar. We do not know whether Ovid actually wrote
such a poem; if he did, it does not survive. But it would be
like him to have done so, to have molded the Getic language
into a Roman verse form on a Roman topic for a Getic audi-
ence. It was a supreme challenge, successfully carried out, if
we can believe the poet. Ovid has, in the fiction if not the
fact of his exile, forced his new world to embrace his old world
(even though he could not force his old world to allow him
to return to it). He reads this poem to an admiring crowd of
Getans—the poet has all the audience anyone could wish—
and one of them comments:

Since you write this about Caesar, you ought to have been
restored by Caesar's command.

[37–38]

He is right, we feel. Ovid should have been allowed to return
to Rome, at least after Augustus's death, but the voice of
humanity and justice, put in the mouth of a barbarian, is not
heard.

Finally, in *Epistulae* 4.14, one of the most interesting
poems in the collection, Ovid puts his *manus ultima* (his fin-
ishing touch) to his creation, rounding off the subject of the
Roman poet in exile, which began in *Tristia* 1.1. The residents
of Tomis are now angry at Ovid because his poems harp on

his desire to live anywhere other than Tomis (15). In the autobiography of exile Ovid's life has returned to its starting point. A poem written early in his career brought down on Ovid the anger of Augustus and sent the poet into exile. Now, at the end of his life, poetry again brings him grief:

> Therefore will I never stop being injured by poetry? Will
> I always be punished by my incautious talent?
>
> [17–18]

But this time no one is at fault and this time the anger is harmless, for the Tomitans have neither Augustus's power nor his desire to hurt Ovid. Indeed they have honored their guest beyond anyone else in their country. They must know, he assures them here, that he hates their country, not themselves:

> My own people, the Paelignians, and my home country,
> Sulmo, could not have been gentler to my sorrows. . . .
> As pleasing as Delos is to Latona, which gave a safe place
> to her in her wanderings, so dear to me is Tomis; it remains to this day hospitable and loyal to me, exiled from
> my native land.
>
> [49–60]

As Ovid develops this portrait—"Ovid among the Goths," Shakespeare called it—he paints a picture of Augustus as well. He does not criticize Augustus, at least not directly. He frequently suggests, in fact, that his punishment is milder than it might have been. But analogies equate Ovid's situation with the animal world, in which the emperor is a hawk, the poet a dove that continues to tremble after escaping its clutches, the emperor is a wolf, the poet a terrified lamb (*Tr.* 1.1.75–78). Ovid speaks of Augustus's clemency (*Tr.* 1.1.73; 2.39ff.) but shows again and again that the man who has pardoned enemies who had plotted against him will not forgive the folly of one who only wrote playful verse (*Tr.* 3.5.31ff.). He suggests that the greater the man, the more willing he is to relent, and contrasts such noble animals as lions, which do not harry the corpse of their prey, with the more vicious wolves and bears in a context that equates the unrelenting Augustus with these wolves and bears. Most telling of all, perhaps, is his portrait of Augustus the god—in particular, Augustus the angry Jupiter—at whose thunderbolts men quake. Other gods are appeased by prayer, but this Jupiter is not (*Tr.* 2.141–42). Safety depends on obscurity, says Ovid, warning a friend to lie low because lightning strikes those who rise to eminence: "he who hides well, lives well" (*Tr.* 3.4.25). The poems paint a picture of an immensely powerful Augustus, a colossus towering over Rome like that which Cassius describes in Shakespeare's *Julius Caesar*:

> Why, man, he doth bestride the narrow world
> like a Colossus, and we petty men
> Walk under his huge legs and peep about
> To find ourselves dishonorable graves,
>
> [1.2]

A man raised to divine status who is, nevertheless, all too mortal.

The poems in *Tristia* 1, 3, 4, and 5 and in the four books of the *Epistulae ex Ponto* make a powerful, if oblique, statement about a poet's collision with a political regime. That collision is the special subject of the *Tristia*'s second book. Addressed to Augustus, this book is Ovid's justification of his life and work. Here he puts his finger on questions as important today as they were nearly two thousand years ago. One is the question of censorship. Does political authority give rulers the right to dictate to writers what they may write and to readers what they may read? Ovid argues (although he could have made a stronger case if he had not let his sense of the comic creep in, even here) that this sort of paternalism is based on a false notion of the relationship between art and life. Literature is not life. There is no reason to assume that reading about adultery leads to the practice of it. A woman who is inclined to wrongdoing will find stimulus in whatever she reads, even something as respectable (and uncouth) as the *Annals* of Ennius (Vergil's epic predecessor). The Roman race, Ovid slyly reminds his reader, was founded on adultery. (Romulus and Remus are, of course, the offspring of the Vestal Virgin Ilia and the god Mars, so adultery and rape are the starting point of Roman greatness [*Tr.* 2.497ff.]).

Augustus did not give in. Neither did Tiberius, who succeeded Augustus in A.D. 14, relent, and the ebullient Ovid was finally crushed and died, in exile, his "Roman soul to wander forever, a foreigner among Sarmatian shades" (*Tr.* 3.3.63–64). Yet Ovid's art survives. His words live on in his poems, his visions permeate our literature, our painting, our sculpture, and our music. Perhaps Augustus did not win after all. Listen to Ovid's words, which ring proudly down the centuries, spoken by one poet about his emperor and through him by the writers of every age about the tyrants who try to control them:

> Here am I, bereft of country, home and you [his family], everything gone that could be taken from me. My art is still my companion and my joy—over that Caesar could not get jurisdiction.
>
> [*Tr.* 3.7.45–48]

III OVID'S LOVE POETRY

The Amores

OVID'S EARLIEST POEMS, THE *AMORES*, WERE, AS WE SAW earlier, rooted in a tradition established by Gallus, Tibullus, and Propertius. The characters, many of the situations, and the language are conventional. The main character in Latin love elegy is the lover, the "Propertius" or "Tibullus" or "Ovid," who speaks the poems in the first person singular. This speaker seems to be the historical poet because of the poems' many apparently autobiographical details, the many references to the Augustan scene, and the poet's apparent sincerity. This sincerity is, however, as Archibald Allen ("Sincerity and the Roman Elegists," *Classical Philology* 45:3 [1950]: 145–60) points out, a matter of style: the basic pose of Latin love elegy is that the man who writes the poems is the lover whose emotions and experiences are depicted. Love, for the poet, is an uncontrollable madness that enslaves, ending only with, or perhaps even surviving, death. A love that has limits, says Propertius, is not true love (2.15.29–30). Thus the relation between lady and lover is that of mistress and slave. Propertius's first poem gives the elegiac stance:

> Cynthia first conquered me with her eyes, unhappy me,
> never struck down by desire before. Then Love cast down
> my ever-disdainful gaze, and planted his feet on my
> bowed head until—shameless one—he taught me to de-

spise chaste girls and to live my life in disarray. A whole
year has passed and my passion rages still, though the
gods in charge are hostile.

[1.1.1–8]

Love crushes the lover to its bidding, and the poem is his cry
of despair, the words wrenched from him by his passion. He
writes elegy because he must.

The elegiac lover, despite his claim to be the historical
poet, has a number of clearly conventional traits. He is always
poor, he has rejected all the traditional Roman professions for
the pursuit of love, and he refuses even to write a more ele-
vated type of poetry, insisting on limiting himself to lowly
elegy. The lady also has conventional traits; she is a beautiful
young woman who occasionally loves the poet in return but
is frequently faithless. She tends to prefer a rich soldier's gifts
to a poor poet's songs. Even when she is willing there are
obstacles—she seems, at least some of the time, to have a
husband or live-in lover who must be tricked if the poet and
she are to meet. The situations depicted are also conventional:
the poet is a soldier in the campaigns of love, he lectures his
mistress about her dress and/or behavior, he serenades her
when he is shut outside and she is inside with someone else.

The imagery in love elegy likewise comes from an estab-
lished tradition. Love is caused by Cupid, who aims an arrow
or thrusts a burning torch at the lover. The lover burns with
the fire of love or is consumed by the wound of love; he is
pale and thin from excessive emotion and lack of sleep. Often-
repeated words for chains and conquering show his servi-
tude. References to watch dogs, guards, and doors evoke his
exclusion from the lady's presence. Such were the ingredients
of love elegy when Ovid set out to write.

The first poem in a Roman poetry book acted as its title
page and introduced the collection. An Augustan Roman

reader would almost inevitably begin a book at the beginning—it was the logical thing to do if you were reading a papyrus roll—and poets designed their opening poems carefully to give readers an idea what to expect. A contemporary opening Ovid's book of *Amores* would have known instantly what to expect when he or she looked at the first column and saw a succession of elegiac couplets in which the poet claims to have been trying to write a poem like the *Aeneid* when Cupid forced him to write love elegy instead:

> I was getting ready to publicize ARMS and VIOLENT WARS in heroic rhythms (for matter must fit meter), making my odd- and even-numbered verses equal—but Cupid sniggered (so they tell me) and stole a foot from every couplet.
>
> [1.1.1–4]

This is a bit of Ovidian byplay pretending that his attraction to epic has been forestalled by a higher power. There is a neat poetic joke here. The first line is a hexameter, suited to those "weightier matters," but the second is shorter by a foot. (See the Metrical Appendix for the foot Cupid stole.) Through this joke Ovid advertises not only that he is writing in the tradition of Tibullus and Propertius and that the poems will be about love rather than important philosophical or political issues but also that they will treat love in a light-hearted and humorous fashion. He urges that Cupid has no jurisdiction over poets and, besides, that he's not in love:

> I have no subject matter for lighter measures, no boy, no long-haired girl—
>
> [19–20]

Cupid responds with a well-aimed arrow and the poet capitulates, bidding his alleged intent to write epic farewell.

Many conventional elements of elegy are obvious here: the emotional, lovesick poet in the grip of an overwhelming passion; a stubborn disinclination to perform in the epic mode (in Ovid's case a disinclination claimed to be forced on him); an encounter with Cupid and his inescapable arrows; and the consuming fires of love. But something has happened to the basic elegiac pose. Propertius's opening word was "Cynthia." Cynthia bowled him over and all the rest followed. In Ovid's first poem there is no girl (we will have to wait till poem 5 to meet Corinna), and love seems to be largely a matter of meter. Where Propertius's poem fuses poet and lover, Ovid's separates them, wittily turning the epic poet into a love poet by degrees in a whimsical and illogical little drama. In essence the poem says: I was writing an epic poem. I had to stop because I found myself writing love poetry instead. But I couldn't write love poetry because I wasn't in love, so I fell in love and now I write love elegy with a passion! Clearly this poet is not going to waste away from genuine emotion.

Ovid is by no means finished with his introduction to love elegy. Propertius sets his scene in one poem, Ovid takes five, each building on the previous ones to create the elegiac love affair à l'Ovide. Poem 1 makes an elegiac poet out of a would-be epic poet. In poem 2 the newly created elegiac poet capitulates to love, allowing General Cupid to triumph over him. Poem 3 fills in one sorely needed detail: the object of his love is female (poem 1 left even that open). As yet, however, the poet has not got very far with her:

> What I pray for is just: let the girl who has recently made me her spoil either love me or give me reason to go on loving her forever. No—I have asked too much. Just let her allow herself to be loved. May Venus hear my many prayers.
>
> [1–4]

Poem 4 fills in another important detail—the girl is married:

> Your husband is going to the same banquet we are; may
> that dinner party, I pray, be the last for your husband,
>
> [1–2]

and there are many obstacles in the lover's path. Poem 5 gets
the lovers to bed—the finishing touch in Ovid's step-by-step
creation of an elegiac poet-lover and an elegiac love affair.
Propertius has a poem on the same theme:

> O happy me! o night that shone for me! and o, you dear
> little bed, blessed by my delights! The number of things
> we said when the lamp was by, the struggles when the
> light was gone! At times she wrestled with me with her
> breasts bare, at others she caused delay by covering her-
> self with her tunic.
>
> [2.15.1–6]

Compare Ovid's opening:

> It was hot and the day had passed its midpoint. I laid my
> limbs to rest on the middle of the bed. The window was
> partly shuttered, partly not, creating the sort of light
> found in woods, like the glow of twilight when the sun
> is leaving the sky, or when night has gone and day not
> yet arrived. That is the light modest girls should have
> offered to them when timid shame wants a place to hide.
> See—Corinna comes, her tunic unbelted, her hair falling
> in two sections over her fair white neck.
>
> [1.5.1–10]

Propertius's is the voice of an excited lover reliving the most
wonderful night of his life. It comes out in spurts; it asks to
be punctuated with exclamation points. We seem to be over-
hearing the poet as he tries to express the inexpressible—
making love with his Cynthia. In *Amores* 1.5 Ovid is not trying
to express the inexpressible. He knows exactly how to say
what he has to say. He is turning a delightful experience into

a marvellous story that requires an audience as urbane and sexually experienced as the narrator. He sets the scene very deftly, creating an erotic atmosphere in the bedroom: sultry midday heat, half light, and suddenly Corinna. Unlike the modest maiden of lines 7–8, Corinna comes ready for action (Roman matrons did not, of course, go visiting with their hair down and their tunics undone). The skirmish over the lady's tunic appears in both poems, but only Ovid goes on to describe, in loving detail, what he saw when Corinna stood naked before him. Nowhere is Propertius so explicit—we have no idea what Cynthia looked like—we see Corinna clearly as Ovid calculatedly leads our eye down her body from shoulders to arms, to breasts, belly, hip, and thigh, at which point he tastefully, and suggestively, stops:

> Why should I report details? I saw nothing unworthy of praise, and pressed her naked body the length of mine. Who does not know the rest? Worn out, we both rested. May such middays come my way often!
>
> [23–26]

Propertius moves from thoughts of love to thoughts of death and of love lasting beyond death. Ovid moves from thoughts of love to thoughts of other equally delightful siestas. He has set his scene for the *Amores*.

Ovid is asking us to see the conventions as conventions, encouraging us to distinguish between the poet and his persona. His first poems explode the pose of sincerity inherited from his predecessors and introduce a new note of play to the genre. The rest of the collection demonstrates how elegy is capable of questioning the reliability of its central figure, the traditional poet-lover, of using the conventions of the genre to laugh at those conventions, and of poking fun at traditional Roman beliefs about life and art and at one or two of Augustus's pet notions.

Ovid may well have invented the device of the "unreliable narrator" who is continually taking up one or another pose. Sometimes he depicts himself as a model of fidelity (although we may think he protests too much when he speaks of his "naked candor" and his "blushing modesty" [1.3]); he affects to be madly in love with Corinna (2.11, and 2.12), yet we see him trying to pick up a new girl a few poems later (3.2). At one moment he claims to be in love with two girls at once (2.10), at another to find every female he meets enchanting (2.4).

Often the pose in one poem deliberately contradicts and subverts that of another. When we read his account of the night he was impotent—the girl was attractive and willing, the lover was willing, but the crucial member, "inert as if touched by poison," was incapable (3.7)—we are doubtless meant to think back to his earlier boast: "no girl has ever been disappointed in my work" (2.10). In poem 2.19 he castigates a stupid husband for allowing easy access to his wife, threatening to lose interest in her if some obstacles are not put in his way; in 3.4 he warns a husband *against* guarding his wife, because it makes her all the more attractive to trespassers. Each wife, the speaker adds piously, should be protected simply by her own virtue. This gives a fine moral ring to 3.4, yet 3.4 and 2.19, taken together, show a blithe disregard for Augustus's legislation concerning marriage and adultery. They make explicit what earlier elegists left shadowy—the status of the beloved. She is unequivocally a married woman, and she and her husband would be subject to Augustus's laws defining adultery and pimping.

Sometimes a poem's end undercuts the pose adopted in its earlier part. 1.7 begins, as do many of Ovid's poems, in the middle of things, with a cry that plunges us immediately into the fiction:

Shackle my hands—they deserve chains—until this frenzy is all past, friend, if any friend be here, for it was madness that moved my reckless arms to beat my mistress; my girl weeps, injured by my crazed hand.

The poem begins at a high rhetorical pitch, and there is nothing to indicate that we should not take it seriously (other than the fact that lovers' quarrels are commonplace). A couple of details (the comparison with the seer Cassandra, undercut as it is made by the reference to her hair ribbons, the belt that stops the poet from ripping Corinna's dress all the way down) may suggest that a cool mind is at work behind the high-flown rhetoric, but Ovid places so much emphasis on the heinousness of the crime and paints the anger on so grand a scale that we are taken in (or nearly so). The last line reveals all. Corinna's hairdo has been ever so slightly mussed, and the whole apology has been a pose—an epicizing of a typical elegiac lovers' quarrel:

> To hide the traces of my awful crime—just put your hair back in its proper place.

Perhaps the best example of Ovid's rhetorical trickery is offered by 2.7 and 2.8. In 2.7 the speaker opens with an outburst of frustration and indignation:

> Am I, then, always to be on trial accused anew? Even though I win, it is a nuisance to have to plead my case so often.

Corinna, it quickly becomes clear, has accused him of being unfaithful. He is indignant; she always misinterprets his slightest gesture, any time he even looks at another woman she is jealous, and now she has actually imagined that he has been playing around with her maid, Cypassis. How monstrous of her! 2.8 opens with an elaborate address to Cypassis. She, it turns out, has been as good in bed with Corinna's lover as at dressing Corinna's hair. The accusation of 2.7 was well founded, and everything the poet said in his defense was a lie. On top of that, he was also misleading us about the real situation in poem 7. The scene did not consist of only Corinna and the lover: Cypassis was present too. The little drama of poem 7 was actually a play for three characters with Cypassis blushing in the background while the lover shamelessly pled his lying case. We have been played for fools.

One of Ovid's great contributions to Latin love elegy, then, is the witty, posturing, self-dramatizing, and often rather obnoxious lover who creates a constantly changing interaction between himself and his audience. Sometimes we laugh at him, sometimes we get infuriated, sometimes we think he is really going too far. At the end of 2.8, for instance, the speaker threatens to tell Corinna the truth about her maid if Cypassis refuses to go to bed with him. "What a cad!" we think, falling again into the poet's trap, for the whole argument is fiction.

Ovid's use of elegiac conventions is often as original as his treatment of the elegiac lover. Any person in a passion is potentially comic to an observer, if not to himself; and the conventions of elegy are, many of them, potentially the stuff of comedy, as the similarities between Roman comedy and Roman elegy perhaps suggest. Ovid's predecessors had played down this aspect of the conventions by delicate handling. Ovid chose to play it up. One of his favorite ways of doing this was to freshen up the well-worn metaphors of love poetry by taking them literally. The metaphor of lovers inflamed by Cupid becomes in 1.1 the little drama complete with dialogue that we have already looked at. In 1.6, wasted from love, as elegiac lovers traditionally are, Ovid's lover claims to be so scrawny that if the door of his lady's house is opened by so much as a crack he will be able to slip in.

The elegiac lover's traditional lecture to his mistress scolding her for dressing too elaborately and using too much makeup also becomes a masterful little drama in Ovid's hands. *His* lover, supposing Corinna to have gone bald from overuse of dyes and curling irons, writes a delightful and infuriating "I told you so" (1.14). Lovingly he describes the glories of the hair that once graced her head—the hair that now lies lifeless on her lap—and wickedly consoles her with the reminder that it will grow back. The hackneyed elegiac convention—if you mess with your hair, you will ruin it—is taken to its logical conclusion in a comic scene featuring an infuriatingly patronizing lover holding forth before his silently weeping mistress. Once again he gets a reaction from the reader. We are ready to kick him for his obtuseness in not realizing that his mistress is upset by his harangue, we think momentarily better of him when it seems he will make amends for his boorishness, and are doubly outraged by his cheerful reminder that the hair will grow back and she will one day no longer need a German wig:

> Calm down and stop making faces! The damage can be made good. After a while you'll be admired for your own hair.
>
> [55–56]

There is tongue-in-cheek comedy here, of course, but there is something else. Ovid offers us glimpses of real life behind the elegiac conventions. In real life, actions have consequences. Part of Ovid's analysis of the conventions entails bringing some of these consequences into the fictional world of elegy.

Before Ovid, elegiac sex had no undesirable effects, except, perhaps, on the feelings of the wretched males. But in real life people like Corinna could get pregnant, despite such birth control as was available. Poems 13 and 14 in Book 2 are very different experiments with the subject of abortion, each an address to Corinna, whose life is in danger because of her

attempt to end her pregnancy. The first asks to be taken
straight; it is a prayer for Corinna's safety, and it sounds sin-
cere, full of topical references to the deities worshipped by
Augustan women. The second is a facetious and amusing
"prolife" statement of the evils of her act:

> What good does it do for girls to stay home, immune from
> war, and to refuse to carry a shield in the savage march-
> ing columns, if without being in a battle they endure
> wounds from their own weapons, and arm unseeing
> hands for their own destruction.
>
> [2.14.1–4]

He goes on to poke fun at the illustrious ancestry of Augus-
tus's imperial line by reminding us that there would be no
Caesars if Venus had aborted Aeneas.

The military metaphor is perhaps Ovid's favorite among
the elegiac conventions, and he plays with it in a number of
ways. In 1.2 he uses the attributes of a solemn Roman triumph
to celebrate the triumph of Cupid, thus trivializing one of the
most venerable Roman customs, deflating the masterful Ro-
man dream of Vergil, and shattering, by comic distortion, one
of the central metaphors of the elegiac genre. The triumph, a
significant Roman institution, the highest honor a general
could receive, was taken so seriously that no one outside the
emperor's family was awarded one after 19 B.C. Ovid's poem
parodies this institution down to the last detail. The triumph-
ing general is Cupid, wearing myrtle instead of laurel, as his
mother, Venus, pelts him with flowers. The triumphal chariot,
drawn by doves (Venus's bird) instead of stallions, has been
thoughtfully provided by Mars, whom Ovid tactfully calls Cu-
pid's stepfather. (One has to call one's mother's lovers some-
thing!) In lieu of captive monarchs, Shame and Conscience
are led along in chains, while Sweet Talk, Error, and Madness
serve as Cupid's soldiers—all this in brilliant parody of

Aeneid 1, in which Jupiter prophesies the end of civil war and the establishment of peace under Augustus. The gates of war will be closed, Jupiter proclaims, and imprisoned inside will be Madness sitting on a pile of weapons, arms bound. Ovid binds Conscience in place of Madness and frees Madness to become one of General Cupid's officers. What is a grand statement of the restoration of order in the *Aeneid* becomes, in the *Amores*, a comic vision of the establishment of disorder. The finishing touch in this reversal is the sly insinuation that, mythologically speaking, Cupid and Augustus are kin (both being offspring of Venus); Ovid urges Cupid to take a leaf from his cousin's book and show the same clemency to his captives that Augustus had boasted from early on. Augustus took pride in the Julian family's supposed connection with Venus. It is one thing, however, to claim a deity as the distant progenitor of one's line, quite another to be confronted with the present-day kinship patterns that result. By bringing an ancient myth into juxtaposition with such everyday realities as cousinship, Ovid makes us question the foundations of Augustan propaganda. Augustus, who wanted only to be celebrated in serious terms by Rome's best poets, can hardly have been pleased by this light-hearted treatment of his mythological family ties, even if, as Ovid says elsewhere, he was probably too busy to read the *Amores* for himself (*Tr.* 2.221–24).

In another poem (1.9) Ovid examines every possibility that the military metaphor affords (to tedious excess, some think) and pokes fun at the military way of life that stood so close to the center of Augustus's prestige. The Roman warrior (who is better qualified to be a warrior than the lover?):

> Every lover is a soldier; Cupid too commands a camp;
> Atticus, you must believe me! *Every lover is a soldier!*
>
> [1.9.1–2]

People may call lovers spiritless, but quite the contrary is true:

I too was lazy, born for unhaltered leisure; writing and
life in the shade had softened my spirit. Love for a beau-
tiful girl spurred me to action and forced me to earn my
keep in the camp of love. Now you can see I am a man
of action, waging nocturnal battles. He who would avoid
sloth, let him love!

[1.9.41–46]

The poem, funny in itself, would have seemed funnier (or at
least more outrageous) to a Roman because it would be out
of tune with his traditional proprieties. Love poems as a genre
were at the bottom of the poetic heap (they are totally private
and they advocate a life of inactivity), and love itself was one
of those things one was expected to outgrow as one matured.
Ovid, perfectly aware of this, coolly claims for love all the
virtues supposedly inculcated by the military life of war and
for the private pleasures of the individual all the values that
Roman tradition and Augustan homiletics reserved for heroic
effort within public spheres.

Through his novel treatment of the lover and of the other
conventions of this kind of poem, Ovid demonstrates that the
Latin love elegy could do much more than had been sup-
posed. One of his major innovations, a first step on the road
that leads to the *Metamorphoses*, is the creation of little stories.
This talent is evident in many of the poems we have looked
at already, including the first poem in the collection, which,
as we saw, turns a metaphor into a little play. The same talent
is evident in his other treatments of the "refusal to write epic"
theme. In 2.1 he again imagines himself writing epic, telling
how the giants Otus and Ephialtes piled Ossa on Olympus
and Pelion on Ossa in order to attack the Olympian gods.

I was working on STORMCLOUDS, and JUPITER, and the
THUNDERBOLT which he was to hurl down in righteous
defence of Heaven, when my girlfriend slammed her

door. I dropped thunderbolt, Jupiter and all. Jupiter van-
ished from my consciousness. Jupiter, please pardon me;
your weapons did me no good. The slamming of that
door packs more thunder than you do.

Once again Ovid literalizes a metaphor and turns it into a
scene. A yet more dramatic version of the "refusal" theme
opens Book 3. This time it takes shape as a funny scene be-
tween two women named Elegy and Tragedy. Elegy arrives
with perfumed hair, stylishly dressed, having the face of a
lover and one foot longer than the other (as befits her meter).
Tragedy sweeps in with wildly flying hair, cloak trailing on
the ground, scepter in hand, wearing the buskins of Greek
tragedy. A delightful confrontation ensues between the two
ladies, each laying claim to the poet's talents. Here, as so
often, Ovid has developed a fascinating scene from a well-
worn theme: the poet's intention to write in a particular vein
is made the subject of a contest between two formidable fe-
males.

One of the most interesting poems in the collection (3.2)
gives us the sights and sounds of a horse race in the Circus
Maximus as background for a little playlet on seduction. In
the first six lines the speaker addresses the girl and sets the
scene—he has no interest in the horses; he is there only be-
cause he wants to be with her. He concludes his first gambit
with:

You look at the races, I look at you; let's each look at what
pleases, and feast our eyes.

[5–6]

Next, he addresses the charioteer whom the girl favors, but
of course the charioteer cannot hear, and the remarks are
actually move number two in the game. Since she likes char-

ioteers, the poet imagines himself as one, masterfully guiding
his horses toward victory until, in his fantasy, he catches sight
of her. All is over:

> If I catch sight of you as I race, I'll slow down and the
> reins will drop slack from my hands.
>
> [13–14]

At this point we catch a glimpse of the girl's reaction.
She has tried to shrink away from him, but, as he points out
gaily, it can't be done, everyone is packed in too closely:

> Why do you shrink away? It's useless! The bench mark-
> ings force us to be close. This is a benefit the Circus has
> by its very nature.
>
> [19–20]

He now becomes officious and addresses first the man on the
girl's right, telling him not to crowd her, and then the man
behind, telling him to get his knees out of her back. Again
we are given just the right details to picture the scene, and
the tone of voice is so skillfully managed that we know exactly
what the man is like; we have seen his type before. Now his
attention comes back to the girl as he affects to notice that the
hem of her garment is dragging. He picks it up and gets a
look at her ankles. This gives him a wonderful opportunity
to scold the cloak for "concealing such nice legs" as well as
other features to which he immediately pays his respects:

> I suspect from these that the rest is pleasing too, those
> beauties lying well hidden beneath your fine dress.
>
> [35–36]

Having mentally undressed her, the lover now changes
his tone, perhaps thinking he has gone too far too quickly or
figuring it best to allow these remarks to sink in before trying
anything else along those lines. He offers to fan her, craftily

suggesting that perhaps the heat is only from his passion, and then he either finds or manufactures an opportunity to touch her when he sees a bit of dust on her dress. (Nothing in the text indicates that the dust is not there, but in an equivalent passage in the *Ars* [1.149–52], he advises the lover to dust her off, whether or not there's anything to dust.)

At last the ceremonial pre-race parade begins and the lover raises his voice. When the images of the gods are carried in procession, he has something to say about each and about the types of people to whom each appeals, lingering, of course, over the image of Venus, who comes last and who (he professes to imagine) has nodded assent to his desires. With another change in tone of voice he worries about the lady's dangling feet. And finally the race begins. The speaker assumes loudly that any charioteer favored by the girl is bound to win and hangs onto this assumption until it is clearly untenable and he has to sputter ignominiously to a stop. He is still undaunted, however. Realizing there is no way their man is going to win, he asks for a rerun, as does the rest of the audience. The race is run again, this time the right man wins, and our expert in seduction thinks he has his victory, too. He reads acquiescence in her eyes:

> She smiled and promised *something* with speaking eyes;
> That's enough for here: pay me the rest somewhere else.
>
> [83–84]

He has won, or so he thinks. We may not be so sure, because he has unwittingly presented himself as the type of conceited boor who might well misread such signals.

Here, in only eighty-four lines, Ovid has given us a vivid picture of a chariot race, of the successive stages of a pickup, and of an amusing, if rather obnoxious, character created (as are the heroines of the *Heroides*) entirely through the speaker's own words. From his earliest works to his last, Ovid seems

to have been fascinated with the ways a story can be told. In
the *Amores*, he experiments (as here) with the ways in which
one speaker can enact a poem apart from any general con-
taining frame. (Later, in the *Metamorphoses*, within a contain-
ing frame, he will orchestrate the "enactments" of many such
speakers into an amazing dramatic whole.) Meantime, he had
begun work on the *Heroides*.

The Heroides

When he wrote the *Amores*, Ovid was working within an
established Roman tradition, as we have seen, and he seems
to have taken the genre as far as it would go: he was the last
of the Roman love elegists. But other realms were open to a
poet interested in continuing with love as his subject and the
short elegiac poem as his verse form. When he set out to write
the *Heroides* Ovid was moving into new territory. He claims
later (*Ars* 3.346) to have invented the poetic letter "unknown
to others," even though Propertius had included a letter from
a woman to her husband in his innovative fourth book (4.3).
Propertius may well have given Ovid the idea for the *Heroides*,
but his epistle from Arethusa to Lycotas, though the subject
is similar, differs greatly from Ovid's composition. For one
thing the scene is contemporary, not mythic; the woman, de-
spite her Greek name, is an Augustan matron (combined with
an elegiac *puella*); and her husband, despite *his* name, is a
Roman soldier fighting on the boundaries of the Roman em-
pire. Furthermore, it is a single experiment; Propertius did
not write a whole book of such letters. Ovid can, then, legit-
imately claim to have created a new literary form with the
Heroides—a claim few Roman poets can make. Certain Greek
precedents for the content of the letters did, however, exist.
They are closely related to the tragic and epic monologue, and
a great deal in Euripides, in Apollonius's *Argonautica*, and in

Vergil's *Aeneid* could have helped Ovid create his portraits of heroines.

The monologue had come to be used especially to explore women's thoughts and feelings. The main difference between a tragic monologue and one of Ovid's *Heroides* is the absence in the epistle of a narrative framework and of any characters other than the heroine. We can assess Dido's outbursts against Aeneas in *Aeneid* 4 in the light of what we have seen of both characters in the first four books of the poem. *Ovid's* Dido (*Heroides* 7) must tell us everything the poet wants us to know for the purposes of the poem. The point of view is hers alone, although Ovid can make her (and his other heroines) tell us more than she is aware of herself.

The *Heroides* are, then, something new in literature. But writing them was a logical next step for the poet of the *Amores*, who enjoyed exploring the possibilities of a genre and who relished the challenge of ringing all possible changes on a limited theme. In the *Heroides* Ovid added a new dimension to elegiac love, took the concept of theme and variation as far as it would go, and recreated for elegy the characters and subjects of epic and tragedy.

The *Heroides* build on the elegiac theme of servitude to love. All of the letter-writers are in a desperate situation because of their love for a man. Language from elegy pervades the letters: the women call themselves "girls," they are "deceived" and "deserted," their men are "slow" and "dilatory." But now the roles are reversed. The women are the slaves to love, the men are fickle. In elegy the lovers quarrel and make up, leave and come back; the speaker despairs at one moment, is ecstatic at another. The book of poems tells a story of different moments in an ongoing, if changing, relationship. The letters of the *Heroides* are static—they have only one moment, and it is always the moment when all is or seems lost. There is, furthermore, an unreality about the seemingly real Au-

gustan world of elegy. For all the poet-lover's posturings we
know that he will not die of love; he will return to love another
day (and to write another poem). Somehow the fictional lives
of the mythical heroines in the *Heroides* seem more real than
the purportedly real lives of the Augustan Roman poets—
another reminder of the fictional nature of anything conveyed
in words.

By transforming the elegiac lover from male to female and
moving him/her out of the world of Augustan Rome into the
world of Greek myth Ovid opened up a new realm, which
we will look at shortly. First we must consider something that
strikes every reader of the *Heroides:* the similarity of the her-
oines and their situations. All have been deserted or left be-
hind by their lovers, eight (Phyllis, Oenone, Hypsipyle, Dido,
Deianira, Ariadne, Medea, and Sappho) by men who have
sailed off never to return; two (Penelope and Laodamia) have
lost their husbands to war, while Hermione has been forcibly
separated from her fiancé. Six (Phyllis, Dido, Deianira, Ca-
nace, Hypermnestra, and Sappho) are about to be killed or to
commit suicide at the moment of writing; two (Canace and
Phaedra) are involved in illicit loves: Canace has committed
incest with her brother, Phaedra would like to do the same
with her stepson. In at least one case Ovid seems to have
gone out of his way to create similarities where none existed
in other versions of the story. Ovid's Hypsipyle is, as Florence
Verducci points out (*Ovid's Toyshop of the Heart* [1985], 56ff.),
a second Medea, a Medea who out-Medeas the true Medea,
even though she is not so depicted in any extant account. It
seems, then, that Ovid strove for the sameness readers have
complained of in the poems. He must have wanted that sense
of similarity; with all of myth to choose from he could have
found more variety than he did and he could have deem-
phasized any similarities. We can assume, then, that Ovid
saw the restrictiveness as a challenge—to himself, to create

as much variety as he could within limited boundaries (much narrower here than in the *Amores*), and to his reader, to read attentively enough to distinguish the nuances. (He used the same approach in the poems from exile, which also require careful reading.) If we do not read carefully, we will probably complain of monotony. What Ovid says of the sea nymphs portrayed on the glorious palace door of the Sun can also be said of the ladies of the *Heroides:*

> They did not all have the same features, nor were they totally different, as is appropriate among sisters.
>
> [*Meta.* 2.13–14]

The heroines bear a strong family resemblance, but each has her own features, which we can see if we look closely enough. (This is especially difficult to do if we are reading a translation, but it can be done if we read with the eyes of the heart and the imagination.)

The more we bring to our reading of the *Heroides*, the more we will take away from it, of course, and, as is usual with Latin literature, what we need to bring if possible is a background in Greek and Latin, especially epic and tragedy. We can read *Heroides* 1, Penelope's letter to Ulysses, or *Heroides* 3, Briseis's letter to Achilles, without reference to the *Odyssey* and the *Iliad*, just as we can read Dido's epistle to Aeneas, *Heroides* 7, with no thought of the *Aeneid* and Sappho's to Phaon with no knowledge of the historical Sappho's poetry, particularly if we read aggressively, alert for each woman's tone of voice. It is easier, though, to see what Ovid is up to if we can compare the self-portrait with the portrait as it appears in other versions. It seems likely that each of the *Heroides* was intended to be seen against the background of one major literary model that it would illuminate and would itself be illuminated by. We cannot be sure of this because many of the likely models are lost, but it is clearly the case with the two Homeric heroines whose letters we shall look at now.

Briseis and Penelope are two of Ovid's most interesting creations, perhaps the most famous of his heroines because of their roles in the *Iliad* and the *Odyssey*. Briseis's letter is a study in the psychology of a slave, as we can see even if we read *Heroides* 3 without reference to the *Iliad*. If we read it with Homer's Briseis in mind, however, we will see that it is more than a study of female psychology; it is also Ovid's version of the *Iliad*, seen from a remarkably different perspective. *Heroides* 3 recreates the events of Books 1–19 of the *Iliad*, reinterpreting some, adding others. The opening couplet sets the scene in *Iliad* 1 after the quarrel between Agamemnon and Achilles: because of the plague sent by Apollo in answer to the priest Chryses' prayers, Agamemnon has had to give up his prize of war, Chryseis, Chryses' daughter, and has seized Achilles' prize, Briseis, to make up for his loss. As Ovid's Briseis puts it:

> The letter you are reading comes from Briseis, who has been seized (*rapta*), the writing by a non-Greek hand is barely legible.
>
> [1–2]

At this point in the *Iliad* the reader is concerned with the confrontation between Agamemnon, the "kingliest," and Achilles, the best fighter, of the Greeks. We pay little attention to Briseis, who is simply a pawn in the controversy. Here in *Heroides* 3 the pawn becomes a real woman. She has feelings; she is in love with Achilles, who should have done something to prevent Agamemnon from walking off with his woman. (We know from the *Iliad* that Achilles almost did attack Agamemnon. He considered killing the king until Athena, on Hera's orders, intervened and pulled him back by the hair.

But it was not love of Briseis that motivated him.) Briseis reads surprise on the face of the heralds who come from Agamemnon to take her:

> Each glancing at the face of the other inquired in silence where our love was.
>
> [11–12]

The *Iliad* knows nothing of this. There the heralds stand silently when they arrive in Achilles' tent because they are terrified and in awe of the great warrior (and this certainly sounds much more plausible than the interpretation Ovid's Briseis gives it). Since then Briseis has been trying to get up the courage to sneak away from Agamemnon's tent. (There is, of course, no suggestion of this in the *Iliad*, where Briseis is not mentioned between Books 1 and 9, and the reader, engrossed in the struggle between Achilles and Agamemnon, gives her no thought.) Lines 23–24 return us to the *Iliad*.

> Patroclus himself, when I was being handed over, whispered in my ear, "Why do you weep? You'll only be here a little while."

Here Ovid adapts an event that takes place much later in the epic. At *Iliad* 19.283ff. Homer's Briseis laments over the corpse of Patroclus because he had shown her kindness when Achilles had killed her family and destroyed her city and had promised that she would be Achilles' wife and return to Phthia with him; "you were kind always," she concludes. This is the one moment in the *Iliad* when Briseis becomes a living, breathing human being with a dreadful past. Ovid's Briseis draws on this moving scene in lines 23–24 and in her account of Achilles' slaughter of her family, which she gives in lines 43–54, but she adds to it material taken from Andromache's speech to Hector in *Iliad* 6.407ff.

There is something horrible in Briseis's adaptation of Andromache's words. Andromache, explaining to Hector that he is all she has since Achilles killed her family, says:

> But Hector, you are my father and my lady mother, you
> my brother and you my young husband;
>
> [429–30]

Briseis, addressing the very man who had killed her brothers and her husband, says, nearly in Andromache's words:

> When I had lost so many, still I had you in recompense,
> you were my master, you my husband, you my brother.
>
> [51–52]

Can one fall lower than to love the killer of one's closest kin? The former princess is not only literally but psychologically a slave. Ovid's Briseis forces us to address an issue that does not come up in the *Iliad*: What will happen to Briseis at the end of the *Iliad*? What becomes of the spoils of war when the men whose spoils they were are killed? Homer does not tell us and we do not ask. Ovid's Briseis looks into the future and there is nothing there for her.

Briseis's version of the embassy to Achilles in *Iliad* 9 differs greatly from Homer's, although it includes the same elements. How different the list of gifts sounds on Briseis's lips: "Seven women from Lesbos skilled in handiwork," says Odysseus in the *Iliad* (9.270–71); "superfluous," adds Ovid's Briseis (*quodque supervacuum est* [35]); Achilles doesn't need women, the implication is, he's got me; he can have whichever of Agamemnon's daughters he wants, "with no bride price," says Odysseus (*Il.* 9.288), "but you don't need a wife," asserts Briseis (*Her.* 3.37). And she contrasts her own fidelity and Achilles' lack of it, accusing him of playing the lyre and of holding a woman in his arms while she is imprisoned in Agamemnon's tent (109–14). She is right, our memory of *Iliad* 9 tells us: when the embassy arrives Achilles is singing of "men's fame" to the lyre (the lyre he had won, as a matter of fact, when he destroyed the city of Andromache's father [186–88]), and when the delegation leaves, Achilles goes to bed with Diomede, a woman he had taken in Lesbos (664). It is amazing how much of the *Iliad* Ovid works into *Heroides* 3: Achilles' threat to leave Troy (*Il.* 1, 9) in lines 57ff.; the Meleager story told by Phoenix (*Il.* 9), 89ff; Agamemnon's vow that he never touched Briseis (107–10; cf. *Il.* 9.274–76, 19.175–77, 258–65).

Heroides 3 is, in a sense, another version of the *Iliad* (to be compared with Ovid's equally strange and suggestive version of the epic given in *Metamorphoses* 12 in Nestor's account of the battle between the Lapiths and the Centaurs). Ovid's idea of epic heroism is very different from Homer's. Although Homer makes us see the futility and emptiness of war at moments in the *Iliad,* he also shows us the heroism and glory that can be won on the battlefield. Ovid has no use for heroes, as we will see when we come to the *Metamorphoses.* In the *Heroides* Ovid seems to question the whole notion of heroism (as Catullus had done in poem 64, his one foray into the world of epic). In *Heroides* 3 Achilles is a poor excuse for a lover and a poor excuse for a hero; his only "heroic" feat is his destruction of Briseis's home and family.

By transferring the figures and concerns of epic to an elegiac setting Ovid comments on both. Ovid's Briseis is a perfect example of what war does to women; she has been emotionally and spiritually destroyed by it. She tries to play a dignified epic role but has no dignity of spirit left. She can only cling desperately to the implausible fiction that Achilles loves her. But Briseis (like the other heroines) is also too small for epic. Her perspective is too limited for her to be a proper mouthpiece for the events of the *Iliad*; she belongs to the elegiac world of the *Amores,* where all can play the game of love and no one gets hurt because it is only a game. Her language is essentially the language of elegy: she wanted to "deceive her guards" like an elegiac puella sneaking out for a clandestine meeting with her lover (17–20); she measures time by the passage of the nights (21–22) in which Achilles should be but is not an eager lover; she has been faithful, he has not (113–16). She measures everything by her (imagined) relationship with Achilles. Such greater issues as honor or heroism do not exist; there are only herself and her predicament. Briseis embodies the basic elegiac motif of the slavery love imposes, but here the metaphor has become a reality. Ovid, who dissected the conventions of love elegy in the *Amores,* reviews them here in the *Heroides* at the same time that he casts a cool, perhaps even cruel, eye on the assumptions of epic.

Ovid's Penelope (*Heroides* 1) is also a remodeling of a Homeric heroine, of course, but in this case a character much more familiar to us than Briseis. In this poem Ovid manages to recreate both the *Iliad* and the *Odyssey* for his own purposes: the first half is Penelope's "Iliad," the second her "Odyssey." Ovid's Penelope is not Homer's Penelope. She is not magnanimous (in the literal sense of "great-souled"); she is an ordinary woman whose husband has not returned after an excessive absence. She is suspicious, jealous, and rather nasty. For all her vaunted fidelity her voice has a sharp edge throughout the letter: Ulysses is lingering, or malingering (57, 66); she has been deserted (7, 8); men are lecherous (75); the dangers of fighting at Troy were less than her imaginings (11); Ulysses was both too forgetful of his family (41) and iron-hearted (58). Even when Penelope chastises Ulysses for his excessive bravery (39ff.) she is making a sarcastic cut, as we realize if we know *Iliad* 10. In that book Diomedes and Odysseus make a night expedition into the Trojan camp, where they first interrogate and kill a Trojan, Dolon, after promising him his safety and then slaughter a number of sleeping Tro-

jans, including Rhesus, whose horses they bring back to the
Greek camp. The whole exploit is not very heroic, and
Diomedes, not Odysseus, is the leader. It is he who does the
killing; Odysseus only pulls the bodies out of the way so the
horses can be brought out. And we can tell from Penelope's
reference to *dolo* (trick [40, 42]) and *somno* (sleep [40]) what
she really thinks of Diomedes' and her husband's "heroism."
Even the suitors are Ulysses's fault:

> all of whom you yourself, disgracefully absent, feed with
> things won by your own blood.
>
> [93–94]

We find no such criticisms from Homer's Penelope.

In the Penelopean "Iliad" Penelope sees herself as the
central character; she is the victim who has borne the suffer-
ing caused by the war; she (that is, her pure love for Ulysses)
is responsible for the victory at Troy:

> Sed bene consuluit casto deus aequus amori.
>   versa est in cineres sospite Troia viro.
>
> [23–24]

> The god, favoring chaste love, had its interests at heart,
> Troy was turned to ashes, my husband safe.

The word order of "Troy," "husband," and "safe" is especially
neatly chosen with *sospite* (safe) and *viro* (husband) surround-
ing Troy, now in ashes. This seems to sum up Penelope's
egocentric view of the world perfectly. How simple everything
is in her perception. Or at least this is the way Penelope would
like to think the world works. But if so, where is Ulysses?
Why is he not safely returned like the other Greek leaders,
she asks, managing to forget that many of the Greeks did not
return at all. Penelope's information about Troy is thirdhand,
told by Nestor to Telemachus and by Telemachus to his

mother, thus liable to distortion, we may feel, quite apart from
the distortions of Penelope's self-centered narrative, the ego-
centricity of which is brought home again as she winds up
her "Iliad" with a description of the site of Troy:

> But *to me* what avail that Troy has been torn apart by the
> arms of you Greeks, and that what once was wall now
> is ground?
>
> [47–48]

As she turns to her "Odyssey" the note of accusation
becomes more strident:

> Although you won, you're not here, and I can not find
> out what reason there is for your delay, or where in the
> world you lurk, you iron-hearted man.
>
> [57–58]

Morandi, which I have translated as "delay," can also suggest
that Ulysses, like the sluggish lover to whom the word is
typically applied, is dallying somewhere. And indeed he is,
as we know from the *Odyssey:* seven years with Calypso and
one with Circe—rather excessive for a man who is supposed
to be hastening home to his wife and family. *Lateas* ("you
lurk" or "you lie hidden"), used of snakes in the grass as well
as people hidden for other purposes, makes clear Penelope's
opinion of the situation. Although she does not let on that
she knows Ulysses is with Calypso, Ovid has her speak in
such pointed allusion to a scene in *Odyssey* 5 that we are likely
to assume that she does know. (Ulysses' stay with Calypso is
one of the facts Homer's Telemachus learns from Menelaus in
Odyssey 4; perhaps Ovid's Telemachus reported this interest-
ing bit of information to his mother, although Penelope does
not say so.) Homer's Calypso tries to persuade Odysseus to
give up on Penelope and stay with her as an immortal, con-
cluding:

I claim to be not inferior to her in form and stature, since
it cannot be that mortals compare with goddesses in form
and beauty.

[*Od.* 5.211ff.]

Odysseus has to decline without offending the goddess—a
difficult task. Fortunately he is the man known to have the
right words on nearly all occasions, as Homer tells us in the
Iliad:

But when he let the great voice go from his chest, and
the words falling thick as the snowflakes in winter, then
no other mortal man could vie with Odysseus.

[*Il.* 3.221–23]

In *Odyssey* 5 Odysseus finds just the right words to make
clear his determination to leave Calypso without offend-
ing her:

Lady goddess, do not be angry at me for this. I know
very well that my thoughtful Penelope would seem a
shadow in beauty and size compared to you; for she is
mortal, you are immortal and ageless. Even so I long
every day to go home.

[*Od.* 5.215ff.]

Ovid's Penelope imagines this very scene, but the Ulysses of
her fancy has not the superb tact of Homer's Odysseus:

While I stupidly fear this [the danger Ulysses may be in],
you may be captured by a foreign love, men's lust being
what it is. Perhaps you're even telling stories about your
wife—how rustic she is, her only refinement carding
rough wool.

[*Her.* 1.75–78]

Ovid's Penelope is clearly more down-to-earth, much less
heroic, and more human than Homer's; she is also another
version of the elegiac heroine familiar to us from love elegy.
Once again the language of elegy abounds. The letter opens
with a cluster of elegiac words (1–8), and ending the poem's
first movement is a vision of Penelope trying to "cheat" the
night by weaving (9–10), just as Cynthia cheated sleep by
weaving or spinning as she awaited the dilatory Propertius
in 1.3.41, thinking that he was with another woman. This is
an elegant elegizing of the epic Penelope's nightly undoing of
the day's weaving in order to put off having to choose one of
the suitors. Another elegiac motif appears in Penelope's pic-
ture of the returned warriors drawing diagrams in wine on
the table of Troy and the battles they had fought there (1.31–
36), a well-known elegiac form of silent communication (*Am.*
1.4.19–20; cf. Tibullus 1.6.19–20), though the subject belongs
to epic (cf. *Aen.* 2.29–30).

Heroides 1 reminds us of something we tend to forget
when we read Homer. Time does not matter in the *Odyssey.*
Although Penelope is not the young girl she was when Odys-
seus left, neither is she an old woman. But in the world of
Heroides 1 (as in the real world) time matters: people get wrin-
kles, people get bad-tempered; many years of coping with a
house full of unwelcome dinner guests, not to mention a
growing boy, a father-in-law, and the perennial servant prob-
lem are enough to ruin the sunniest disposition. The reunion
that Homer describes in Book 23 of the *Odyssey* could not
possibly take place between the Ulysses and Penelope of
Heroides 1. Ovid diminishes the epic Penelope but makes her
more human, more like us.

At the same time, by making Penelope an elegiac heroine,
Ovid comments on the conventions of elegy, showing how
inadequate they are to real life. Penelope thinks of herself as

a puella (3), but she must be at least thirty-five, maybe forty
years old. By the end she envisions herself as an *anus*, an old
woman:

> Certainly I who was a girl when you left will, even if you
> came home immediately, seem to have become an old
> woman.
>
> [115–16]

Delay takes on a new meaning when it means twenty years,
not a few hours. The old woman may suggest something else
as well. She is another character from elegy, the "bawd" who
looks out for the puella's interests with rich gentlemen
(against the interests of the poverty-stricken poet-lover). (See
Amores 1.8 for the old woman Dipsas, or Tipsy.) She is also
the woman whose beauty has faded and who no longer at-
tracts men. In the *Ars* the inspired seer urges women to give
favors while they can, for:

> There will be a time when you who now exclude lovers
> will lie, an old woman, cold, deserted through the night.
>
> [*Ars* 3.69–70]

This may throw interesting light on Penelope's famous chas-
tity. Penelope has done without sex for twenty years, and she
is frustrated. Certainly her formulation of the suitors' wooing
is aggressively erotic: what Grant Showerman translates in
the Loeb Classical Library *Heroides* as the suitors "a wanton
throng, come pressing about me, suing for my hand" (*turba
ruunt in me luxuriosa proci* [88]) is more sexually suggestive
than he implies. *Luxuriosa* means unbridled or wanton; it also
alludes to fertility, luxuriance, and rankness. *In me ruunt* can
be translated as "rushes at me" or even "into me." Penelope
may well be the sex-starved, sex-obsessed woman Howard
Jacobson calls her (*Ovid's Heroides* [1974], 268–73). (She is not
unlike Ovid's Sappho, who is a pathetic case of an older

woman desperately trying to win back the interest of an attractive young man.)

   If *Heroides* 1 and 3 are a reasonable sample, as I think they are, Ovid's heroines differ significantly from each other despite their similarities, and Ovid has accomplished an impressive feat by taking the short elegiac verse form into new territory.

The Ars Amatoria

   By the time Ovid had completed the *Amores* he may have felt he had done all that could be done with love elegy as such. Nevertheless, the theme of love continued to appeal to him, and he struck out in a new direction with it. Vergil had moved from short pastoral poems, to didactic, to epic. Ovid probably had this progression in mind when he decided to write a didactic poem on love; in any case it was a natural progression for a poet who had achieved success in one genre to move up in the generic hierarchy to a verse form that was generally thought to be more serious, more elevated, and more difficult.

   In the twelfth century Heloise, in a letter to Abelard, called the poet of the *Ars* "that master of sensuality and shame" (*The Letters of Direction*, letter 5); in the fourteenth century Petrarch called the mind that produced it "lascivious, lecherous, and altogether mulierous" (*De vita solitaria*). Most readers will not, I think, respond to the *Ars* as did these two scholars, but they may be somewhat baffled as to how to take it. A reader approaching the *Ars* for the first time—without any of the expectations a Roman would have had from a knowledge of the conventions of the genre—is likely to be amused by parts of the poem, infuriated by other parts, and curious about what Ovid is up to. The poem contains a great deal of advice, some of it sound. All of us, at least after our

teen years, can applaud his advice to be lovable if you want
to be loved (2.107), for beauty is not enough and will fade.
Classicists (like myself) will approve his advice to learn two
languages well (2.122). His warning to men to be neat and
clean but not foppish (1.513–24) sounds sensible, as does his
recommendation that women be elegant but not overdressed
(3.129–34). He tells men not to boast about the affairs they
have had or to claim those they haven't (2.625–40). We all
know people who have not taken this advice and wish they
had. Older women will probably be impressed with his per-
ception that they often make better lovers than the young
(2.675–702); all women will be pleased with his insistence that
the pleasures of love be shared by both partners (2.683–88).
On the other hand, any woman is sure to be infuriated by his
claim that women actually like to be raped (1.673–78) and by
his recommendation that they fake orgasm (3.797ff.), and
nearly everyone today will be put off by the lack of sincerity
advocated throughout. Throughout the *Ars*, Ovid's professor
proposes calculation, lying, manipulation, and pretense.

The *Ars* is, in many ways, the didactic counterpart of the
Amores. A Roman picking up such a poem in Ovid's day
would have had certain expectations about didactic, shaped
in part by the Greek didactic tradition and in part by the
Roman tradition. Hesiod, the younger contemporary of Ho-
mer who wrote the *Works and Days*, the *Theogony*, and a cata-
logue of women, was regarded as the father of didactic and
was taken by Callimachus in the third century b.c., and later
by his Roman adherents, as the proper model for the new
kind of poetry. Aratus, a contemporary of Callimachus, wrote
a versified treatise on the heavens, the *Phaenomena*, which was
much loved by Romans and was translated by several, in-
cluding Cicero. Nicander (second century b.c.?) wrote didac-
tic poems on poisonous snakes and antidotes, poems that
Roman readers knew well. Ovid may have made a sophisti-

cated and oblique allusion to Nicander's pairing of poisons
and antidotes when he added his *Remedia*, an antidote to the
teaching of the *Ars*, to his didactic collection. Surviving, or
partially surviving, didactics of the Augustan Age are Marcus
Manilius's *Astronomica* on astronomy and Grattius's *Cynegetica*
on hunting, but Ovid mentions didactic poems on dice-play-
ing, the shape and use of balls, the arts of swimming and
hoop-rolling, and various other subjects (*Tr.* 2.471ff.).

Clearly, didactic appealed to Roman poets and, presum-
ably, to Roman readers; but most of the surviving poems,
while they may be interesting, are not great works of art, and
it seems unlikely that those that do not survive (dice-playing
or swimming, for example) reached great heights. But two
Roman poets before Ovid did write masterpieces of didactic,
and it is these whom Ovid intended to rival when he wrote
the *Ars*. Ovid's poem pretends to be written in the serious
didactic tradition of Lucretius's *De rerum natura* and Vergil's
Georgics. Both of these poems expound a view of life the
speaker passionately believes in and thinks is essential for the
reader to learn in order to live well. On this account, he is
rather like a preacher giving a sermon or an orator pleading
a case; and, just as a good preacher or a good orator varies
the tone to fit the subject and to keep the listener's attention,
so the didactic speaker modulates his tone and intensity as
he moves from topic to topic. His conviction sweeps us along
and, while we are reading the poem, seems to confer validity
on what he says. This persona is the didactic equivalent of
the putatively sincere lover of Roman elegy whom we looked
at earlier in the chapter.

Didactic structure, language, and themes are also, to
some extent, predictable. The speaker exhorts his audience
to pay attention, he commands, he questions, he proves
points by his own experience ("I have seen," "I remember");
he shapes his argument in orderly fashion with careful artic-

ulation ("at first . . . in addition . . . furthermore . . . now I shall"), imagining the progress of the poem as a sea journey or chariot race with a goal in sight but occasionally steering off course to digress into the mythological or historical past to elucidate the present.

Ovid's poem clearly relates to this tradition. The speaker insists on being taken seriously. He emphasizes the need for understanding and hard work and, aware that his recommendations will not be easy to follow, he cajoles and exhorts the listeners for their own good. He uses the articulating devices I mentioned above to give a clear structure to his course:

> In the beginning, work to find something to love, you who come to battle now for the first time, a new warrior. The next task is to win the girl who pleases you, the third to make love last a long time.

> [1.35–38]

Compare the opening of Vergil's *Georgics*, which includes the subjects of all four books:

> What makes happy crops, under what star it is suitable to turn the earth, Maecenas, and to join vines to elms, what care is needed for cattle, what tending for sheep and goats, what experience for thrifty bees, I shall set out to sing.

> [1.1–4]

Ovid moves from his first to his second book with a neat summary of what has been accomplished and what remains:

> So far my Muse, carried on uneven wheels, teaches where to choose something to love, where to spread your nets. *Now* I tackle a project requiring outstanding skill: by what arts she who has pleased you is to be caught.

> [1.263–66]

This proposal is actually much neater as a plan than it turns out to be in practice, for Ovid immediately moves into myth to prove that all women can indeed be caught. Only after citing three examples of perverted love: Byblis's passion for her brother, which he will take up again in *Metamorphoses* 9, Myrrha's love for her father (*Meta.* 10), and Pasiphae's for the bull, and carefully pointing the moral in the didactic manner:

> So then, don't doubt that you have hope of all girls;
> scarcely one of many will say no to you,
>
> [*Ars* 1.343–44]

does he get on with instructions for capture. The poet also includes a number of didactic digressions: from mythology—Daedalus and Icarus, 2.23ff.; Ulysses and Calypso, 2.123ff.—from Roman legend—Romulus and the rape of the Sabine women, 1.101ff.—and even, rather disconcertingly, from history, in the shape of prophecy—the future triumph of Gaius, 1.177f. He urges his listener to pay attention (1.267), he gives orders (1.51), he asks rhetorical questions: you ask whether you should seduce the maid? (1.375), and he emphasizes the need for hard work (1.35) and knowledge (1.50).

Everything about the poem's form indicates that we are to read the *Ars* as a didactic poem in the serious tradition of Lucretius and Vergil. But, of course, we cannot read it seriously. Ovid has chosen a topic that is frivolous by anyone's standards, shocking by the standards Augustus was trying to revive in Rome, and he has treated it in deadpan fashion—soberly and from all angles, as if it were an important philosophical or ethical question, such as the nature and pursuit of virtue. There is thus an initial incongruity between the poem's subject and its form.

The first thirty-four lines introduce the poem and the

speaker. The opening couplets emphasize the practical didactic character of the work; the word *ars* (art, skill, technique) is used four times:

> If anyone in this populace does not know the art of loving, let him read this and, having read my poem, love as an expert. By art swift ships move with sail and oar, by art light chariots move, by art must love be ruled.
>
> [1.1–4]

This is to be a manual, a handbook. Lines 5–18 add a new dimension: they hook the poem firmly into the epic tradition with references to Automedon, Achilles' charioteer; Tiphys, the helmsman of the Argo, which was the first ship ever to sail; Chiron, the centaur who was Achilles' tutor; Achilles himself; and Hector. Then, however, the speaker moves out of myth into the agricultural world of the *Georgics*:

> But, nevertheless, the bull's neck is burdened with the plough, and high-spirited horses champ the bit with their teeth,
>
> [19–20]

while the next two couplets plant him firmly in the world of love elegy with its wounds and its torches:

> And love will yield to me, however much he wounds my heart with his arrows and shakes and hurls his torch; the more he pierces me, the more violently he burns me, the better avenger I shall be of the wound he has made.
>
> [21–24]

The next three couplets point to Hesiod and the long tradition that began with his claim to have met the gods of poetry: Hesiod, *Theogony* 22ff.; Callimachus, *Aetia* prologue; Ennius, *Annales* prologue; Vergil, *Eclogue* 6.3ff.; Propertius 3.3.13ff. (cf. 2.1.3, 4.1.133–34); Horace, *Odes* 4.15. This "seer" (*vates*, the word that had come to be used for inspired poets tackling great themes) is not inspired, he's experienced—sexually! What does this tell us about Ovid's preceptor of love? Let us follow him through the proem, as he gives his credentials. If we look at them with care we will see how Ovid intends us to take him. The first couplet gives us an idea of his character, supremely assured and rather pompous:

> If anyone in this populace does not know the art of loving, let him read this and, having read my poem, love as an expert.

Already the implicit assumption of any "how to" handbook, whether Roman or modern, that the speaker will be a reliable guide is shaken, only to be further shaken by his dubious premise that love is a skill like seamanship or chariot driving and can be mastered. Mastered, that is, if well taught. And how can it not be well taught by so accomplished a professor—one who, according to his own account, is a technician of heroic proportions, the equivalent, in his field, of Tiphys or of Automedon?

In the next stage of his argument the speaker redefines preceptor and love without realizing it. The preceptor of love, who was a professor of a science just a moment ago, now presents himself as the tutor of the love god, Cupid, and thus the epic equivalent of the centaur, Chiron, tutor to the young Achilles. Both boys were hard to discipline, but since Chiron succeeded:

> He who so often terrified his allies as well as his enemy is believed to have been in terror of an old man; those hands which Hector was destined to feel, he offered, when his tutor asked him to, under orders, for beating,
> [1.13–16]

so will his successor. The terms used to describe Cupid's powers of resistance, his ability to wound, pierce, and burn (not to mention that he is a god and hence not really susceptible to human control), make it abundantly clear that our preceptor's claimed domination of "love" is a delusion, as must be also, therefore, his credentials as guide. Even less reassuring, since he professes to speak as a poet, is his bland assumption that experience without inspiration is enough. What he is going to tell us, he implies, will be true because he has first-hand experience, whereas inspired poets like Hesiod have been either ignoramuses or liars. So much for that creative power of mind and heart that older poets call the Muse and more modern ones the Imagination.

In brief, Ovid has sketched for his speaker, the "Ovid" of the poem, an amusing but pedantic fool. Like the speaker in Jonathan Swift's "A Modest Proposal," he has virtually no ethical sense and little self-knowledge. Both are convinced that a rational "method" can solve life's problems, whether it be overpopulation in Ireland or love in Rome. So the first thing Ovid has done is to take the stuffing out of the didactic narrator. We cannot depend on him as we could on Lucretius's or Vergil's instructor to help us see the way things are. He is a comic figure whose tone becomes inappropriately more sober and reflective as his message becomes more outrageous. Is it a good idea for the young lover to get to know the maid of the lady he is pursuing? Yes, yes—a maid can be very useful in arranging meetings, speaking favorably of the lover, and so on. Then might it be an even better idea to begin by seducing the maid? Well, no. On the whole, the professor does not recommend it, because you cannot be sure what effect it will have on her; it might make her less zealous on your behalf with the lady. All things considered, it seems advisable to get the mistress first and then go for the maid, if you find her attractive (1.375–86).

Since selecting a woman for seduction is an exacting science, the speaker is businesslike about it. We should choose in daylight so we can get a clear look at the goods, just as we would if we were looking at gems or fabrics. Poor light can conceal faults. (This is just the kind of advice that old Cato gives to a man interested in buying a farm in his handbook on agriculture; the astute Roman does not want to be taken in.) Select a mistress as you would select a cow. Not that such detachment is always easy. Our professor has not, he admits, quite mastered it himself. But it is nonetheless indispensable for the greatest feat the rational lover must be prepared to perform. So great a feat that his verse quickens as he thinks of it:

> Why do I dally among minor matters? My spirit presses on to greater ones. I sing great things; listen, crowd, with all your heart! Our struggle here is uphill, but all excellence is hard to reach. A difficult task is demanded of my art.
>
> [2.535–38]

Four lines prepare us for something momentous. Then the great deed is unveiled: "you must patiently put up with a rival."

Nothing is sacred to our instructor—not even the idea of lucky and unlucky days, which he appropriates from Hesiod (*Works and Days* 383ff.) and Vergil (*Georgics* 1.204ff.). In the battle of wits, otherwise known as a "rational" love affair, where the woman's aim is to get as much as she can and the man's to give as little as he must, anniversaries of national disasters are to be regarded as lucky days. Why? Because the stores are closed and you cannot be expected to bring a present! Even worse, the speaker shows his total vulgarity of spirit by reapplying to the work of getting the girl on the cheap (that is, without presents) one of the most famous passages of the *Aeneid*. In Book 6 the Sibyl tells Aeneas how difficult it is to leave the Underworld alive. Going down is easy, she warns, but getting out again—"this is the task, this the toil" (*hoc opus, hic labor est* [*Aen.* 6.129 = *Ars* 1.453]). The best-known "wisdom" of the ancient world, "know thyself," long associated with the oracle of Apollo at Delphi and with Socrates, meets with equally short shrift (2.501). As reinterpreted by our guide, it means: know your own strengths and flaunt them—sing if you have a voice, talk if you are a good conversationalist, and so on. In 3.771ff. he even adapts it to choosing the most flattering positions for making love, not a revision of the old wisdom likely to endear Ovid to Augustus, who associated Apollo with his success at the Battle of Actium against Antony and with the Augustan peace.

Ovid has given his speaker a second and more dangerous role. Through the mouth of his apparently self-absorbed spokesman, like Shakespeare through the mouth of the fool in *King Lear*, Ovid manages to get some dangerous things said. Advising lovers to avoid harsh words he asserts that quarreling is for those who are legally married: "This befits wives: quarrels are the dowry of a wife" (2.155), and "The law wasn't your authority for getting into bed together" (2.157), thumbing his nose at Augustus's moral legislation. He also seems to relish the demeaning circumstances that public buildings named after Augustus and his family have become trysting places and cites as good hunting grounds four porticoes: that of Octavia, Augustus's sister, that of Marcellus, Octavia's son and Augustus's grandnephew, son-in-law, and intended heir until his death at an early age, that of Livia, Augustus's wife, and that of Agrippa, his good friend and later son-in-law. (Certainly he could have found many places less intimately connected with Augustus if he had wanted to.) The theater is one of the better places for woman-hunting, his spokesman remarks, and then, in the traditional manner of didactic searching the past for the origins of a current practice, exclaims: "You, Romulus, were the first to upset the games" (*primus sollicitos fecisti, Romule, ludos* [101]), with a pun on sollicitos, for another translation would be "you were the first to make games an occasion for fear," as if this were an impressive achievement. Roman writers were fond of claiming to be the first to do something: Lucretius speaks of reaching the Muses' haunts, "trodden by no one's foot before," drinking from an "untouched spring," plucking "new flowers" for a wreath "from a source from which the Muses have wreathed no one's head before" (*De rerum natura* 1.926ff.), and Vergil says:

> I delight in walking in mountains where no one before me has left the traces of his chariot wheels as he turns aside to Castalia by a gentle slope.
>
> [*Geo.* 3.291ff.]

This claim of originality often takes the form it has here in the *Ars:* "x was the first to" do something significant. It is a shock to find Romulus congratulated for his invention of kidnapping women at the games. The professor goes on to describe the rustic setting (the picture is clearly meant to contrast with present-day elegance) and the kidnapping, orchestrated by Romulus, of the Sabine women who had come to watch the games:

> You alone, Romulus, knew how to give soldiers benefits; if you give me these benefits, I will be a soldier. Indeed, as a result of that custom, even now, theatrical performances are dangerous to the beautiful.
>
> [1.131–34]

Through his mouthpiece, Ovid laughs at Roman nostalgia for a more innocent past when chastity and modesty reigned. As the instance of the Sabine women hints, the past was no different from the present except in being more brutal. And the "benefits" alluded to would perhaps remind a Roman of Augustus's current difficulties in getting recruits for the army. (The emperor had been forced greatly to improve retirement benefits in order to lure more young men into the military.)

Ovid's treatment of the other major Augustan nostalgic theme, the Golden Age, shows him at his most characteristic, as we saw in chapter 2. A great deal of lip service was being paid in his time to the idea of a long ago age of peace and simplicity that Augustus was often said to have recreated. We find the Golden Age in all of Vergil's works, in Horace's *Odes*, in Tibullus and Propertius. Both Vergil (*Aen.* 6, 8) and Horace (Odes 4.2) specifically link the Golden Age of the distant past under Saturn with the present or future golden age under Augustus. Ovid is too clear-sighted and too cynical to be impressed by notions of recreating past simplicity—you had only to look at Augustus's public building program to realize that simplicity was not really at issue. Ovid, being Ovid, does not set out a contrast between the ideal and the real as Horace might have done; instead, he glorifies the real: "Before, there was rude simplicity, now Rome is golden, possessing the wealth of the conquered world. . . . Old-fashioned things may please others, I congratulate myself for having been born now. This age is suited to my tastes" (3.113–22). In another mood, he says:

> Golden, truly, is the present age; for gold most honors are sold, by gold love is won. Even you, Homer, even if you come accompanied by the Muses, it'll be *out you go Homer*, if you haven't brought anything.
>
> [2.277–80]

Vergil hints, perhaps, at the discrepancy between Golden Age simplicity and golden Rome in *Aeneid* 8, where, in his survey of the site of Rome from earliest times to the Augustan Age, he offers, without comment, a contrasting vision of three

ages: the long ago Golden Age, where gold signified peace
(319–27), Evander's Rome in its poverty and simplicity
(throughout the book), and Augustan Rome, where gold rep-
resents luxury (348; cf. 715ff.). Ovid does more than hint.
Greek mythology was a treasure house of tales into which
every Roman poet dipped either to relate his poetry to his
great Greek predecessors or to make sense of the universe by
finding parallels or contrasts in the past. But the heroes of
Greek myth can no more escape the scalpel of the Doctor of
Love than could the Roman political and poetic establishment.
In the *Ars*, myth proves the poet's points again and again.
Rape is acceptable to women—compare Phoebe and Hilaira
raped by Castor and Pollux (1.679–80) or Deidamia raped by
Achilles (1.697–706). Watch out for quarrels—think of Eury-
tion and the drunkenness that led to the battle of Lapiths and
Centaurs (1.591–94). Friends cannot be trusted with your girl
despite the examples of Patroclus, Pirithous, and Pylades
(1.743–46). Mental capacity is more important than looks—
witness Ulysses who, though he was not good-looking, was
eloquent and so won over the goddess Calypso (2.123–24).
Absence makes the heart grow fonder—note Phyllis and De-
mophoon, Penelope and Ulysses, Laodamia and Protesilaus
(2.351–56); excessive absence is dangerous—think about Me-
nelaus and Helen (2.357–72). For the dangers of jealous
women, see Medea and Procne (2.381–84), of women
scorned, see Clytemnestra (2.397–408), and so on. The pro-
fessor obviously thinks that his mythological parallels give
legitimacy to his modern teachings. But there is a reductive
effect at the same time, and it works two ways. First, the
heroic figures dwindle, as they do in the *Heroides*. Ordinarily,
when we think of Andromache, for instance, we think of her
as Homer presents her in *Iliad* 6 and Vergil in *Aeneid* 3: a lov-
ing wife and mother, an example of what war does to women.
Before the events Homer describes in the *Iliad*, Andromache

has already lost almost everything—family and home—all destroyed by Achilles. In the course of the *Iliad* she loses her husband, and she will soon lose her only son. In Vergil's account, she lives on, a mere shell of her former self, wholly given over to the past.

What does Ovid's spokesman make of Andromache? He says that Hector's not minding her exceptional height is proof that lovers should not worry about physical flaws in the beloved (2.645–46). He says, in a discussion of foreplay, that Hector was not successful only in battle (2.709–10). He says that Andromache's plain dress is evidence that the women of old, unlike women today, were not very elegant—a fault there was no one to notice, however, for her husband was only a rough soldier (3.109–10). He says that women should not be melancholy like Andromache or Tecmessa, neither of whom would he ever choose for his lover; indeed, only the fact that they had children can convince him that they made love with their husbands (3.519–20). And he says that Andromache's excessive height was the reason she never made love with Hector by riding him like a horse—this amid advice to show off your charms to advantage when choosing a position for sexual intercourse. Andromache has not just been reduced from a great tragic heroine to an ordinary woman, she has been shrunk to a collection of traits (height, rusticity, sadness), at which the professor smirks. We have to know the tradition to see what Ovid through this mouthpiece has done with it. Andromache *was* tall, no doubt, as women of the heroic age were; she *was* melancholy, of course, for she had lost everything; her dress *was*, very likely, not what a fashionable Augustan lady would wear. The professor reduces nearly everything to its lowest common denominator and then sneers.

Yet, as mentioned above, the effect is double. If *he* reduces Andromache, *she* reduces him and all that he pretends

to know about "love." What have he and his playgirl to do
with those images of loyalty and fidelity—Laodamia and Pro-
tesilaus, Penelope and Ulysses, Andromache and Hector—
images of an ideal to which human nature has always aspired
(even if rarely attained) and will not willingly let go? What,
for that matter, do he and his mistress have to do with those
to whom love in its infinite irrationality has brought only
hatred, jealousy, and mistrust—dread images of what we
must fear about ourselves: Agamemnon and Clytemnestra,
Jason and Medea, Menelaus and Helen. Beside such giant
projections of what we have it in us to become, our professor
and his girlfriend, together with the thesis that love is simply
a display of erotic technique, fade into insignificance. Mean-
while, Ovid has managed a feat that no one before him had
succeeded with so well: making a poem on the grand scale
out of the most frivolous of subjects.

Our sense of the magnificent incongruity between the
subject and the style of the poem increases if we realize how
much Ovid has taken from the works of Vergil, especially the
Georgics. There are so many allusions to the *Georgics* in the
Ars that it is clear Ovid wanted us to have it in mind as we
read. I have mentioned a few; there are many more. Book 1
is full of them: the exhortation to work hard at 1.35 takes us
right into the world of the *Georgics*, where toil is piled on toil
without respite. But you must study before you go into action
(line 50ff.), and much of the *Georgics* is devoted to the farmer's
need for knowledge, without which his physical exertion will
be in vain. Among other things he must understand the soil
before he can know how to plow it and what to plant in it,
for it is a fact of nature that certain soils are suited to certain
crops—you cannot expect all things to grow everywhere. One
of the most brilliant passages in the *Georgics*, the so-called
Laudes Italiae, or "Praises of Italy" (2.136ff.), finds a new twist
in the *Ars*.

> But neither the forests of the Medes, the wealthiest land,
> nor the beautiful Ganges and the river Hermus, turbid
> with gold, can vie with Italy in praise

sings Vergil in one of his most optimistic moods. He goes on
to extol its virtues—eternal spring, natural fertility, the ab-
sence of dangerous animals, the presence of great cities and
great men. Italy has it all and needs nothing from abroad.
But he makes no mention of women (not surprisingly); that
is left for Ovid. His novice in love will not have to sail to
foreign lands to find a girl (as Perseus had to do to find An-
dromeda or Paris to find Helen):

> Rome will give you so many and such beautiful girls that
> you will say, "this city contains whatever there is in the
> world."
>
> [*Ars* 1.55ff.]

Ovid's bee simile (1.95–96) comes from *Georgics* 4.162–69; the
cows and horses of lines 279–80 take us back to Vergil's dis-
cussion of the sexual urge of mares in *Georgics* 3.266ff., and
so on. Ovid's poem is so full of specific allusions to Vergil
that one imagines part of his purpose in writing it must have
been to show that the genre of didactic lends itself to a very
different manner of treatment from that which it found in
Vergil's hands. This is not to suggest that Ovid was trying to
undercut the *Georgics*, only that he was already doing in the
Ars what he was about to do on a grand scale in the *Meta-
morphoses*—playing off the earlier poet in order to show that
great poetry need not be written in the style and vein chosen
by his predecessor.

IV THE METAMORPHOSES

THE PROCLAIMED THEME OF OVID'S GREATEST AND MOST AM-
bitious work is change, "forms changed into new bodies,"
with a suggestion that the poem's form was changed even as
it took shape: "Gods, inspire my undertaking (for you have
changed it too)":

> In nova fert animus mutatas dicere formas
> corpora; di, coeptis (nam vos mutastis et illas)
> adspirate meis.
>
> [*Meta.* 1.1–3]

Ovid begins his *Metamorphoses*, then, with a reversal of his
demotion from epic to elegiac poet in *Amores* 1.1 expressed in
a more dignified way, as suits the loftier genre he has in hand.
Metamorphosis is the subject and the essence of the poem,
which transforms everything it touches—both its content and
its structure. The *Metamorphoses* is like no poem written before
it, although virtually everything in it can be found elsewhere.

When we think of the *Metamorphoses*, we tend to think of
certain wonderful stories—the stories of Pyramus and Thisbe,
of Narcissus, Medea, Pygmalion, Orpheus—all these and
many more are likely to linger in our memories long after we
have read them. All through the Middle Ages and into the
Renaissance the *Metamorphoses* was generally read as a collec-
tion of fables, although the sixteenth-century poet Ariosto
recognized its principles of organization and incorporated
them in his *Orlando furioso*. All of the major stories can be

extracted and read by themselves, and they stand up well to such excision, as we see when we run into them in Latin textbooks and mythology handbooks. But we are left with a great deal of rubble once we have extracted the "good bits," and we may well wonder why Ovid included it. It is tempting to linger over Ovid's best stories (his studies of passion-driven women like Medea, Scylla, and Myrrha, his accounts of failed artists like Arachne and Orpheus, his tales of devoted married couples like Deucalion and Pyrrha, Cadmus and Harmonia, Baucis and Philemon, Ceyx and Alcyone), but these are very readable in Latin or in English and many of them have been well treated in books readily available in any library. Since this is so, my major concern in this book will be with aspects of the poem that tend to give people trouble—both its structure, including transitions between stories, and its less appealing tales. But I shall begin with a gem of a story that serves as a transition from the tales of divine love and rape that make up Book 2 to the stories connected with the house of Cadmus that make up Book 3.

The Story of Europa

At the end of Book 2 (836–75), Ovid tells the story of Europa and Jupiter. It is only forty lines long, but it is a beautiful example of Ovidian artistry. The subject, female mortal pursued by lustful male god, is of course one of Ovid's favorite subjects in the first books of the poem. The story of Europa is the fifth of this kind, coming after the tales of Apollo and Daphne, Jupiter and Io, and Pan and Syrinx in Book 1 and Jupiter and Callisto in Book 2 (not to mention the stories of Apollo and Coronis and Mercury and Herse, though in these the women are, apparently, willing). When we get to Ovid's account of the rape of Europa, we already have a good idea of what kind of story it is likely to be, even if we do not know the myth. Ovid slips the episode's subject, love, and its location, Phoenicia, into his first sentence. Jupiter, without telling him why, sends Mercury to Sidon to drive the king's cattle down to the seashore. Mercury obeys, then vanishes from the poem. A slight change of grammar, however, gives us a new piece of information. In the command, Jupiter refers to the royal herd:

> Drive to the shore the royal herd you see feeding at a
> distance on mountain grass;
>
> [2.841–42]

When the command is carried out, the royal herd has become a herd of bullocks (masculine plural rather than a collective noun, neuter singular), and they arrive at the shore in the line that introduces the king's daughter. The syntax illustrates the scene: bullocks and princess sharing a line and a place.

All of this is preliminary scene-setting. Ovid begins the narrative proper with an editorial comment—majesty and love do not go well together—and points up the contrast between the power of Jupiter, expressed in three ways, and the undignified nature of the imposture he adopts, again put in three ways:

> Majesty and love do not go well together, nor can they
> exist in the same place. Putting off the gravity of king-
> ship, the father and ruler of gods (he whose right hand
> is armed with the triple-pronged thunderbolt, he who
> shakes the world with his nod), put on the shape of a
> bull and, mingling with the bullocks, mooed and walked
> in his beauty over the tender grass.
>
> [846–51]

Every detail contributes to the absurdity of Jupiter and proves that indeed majesty and love do not go together. One detail points to the future, the adjective *formosus,* which I have translated "in his beauty." Because he is beautiful, the god is dangerous. This is comedy—we have to laugh at Jupiter—but his power is real, and mortals are weak, and terror lurks just out of sight. The next few lines describe the Jupiter-bull in exquisite detail:

> His color was that of snow that no heavy foot has trodden and no rainy south wind has turned to slush, the muscles swelled on his neck, the dewlap hung down on his shoulders. His horns were small, to be sure, but you would wager they were handmade and more gleaming than pearls. His forehead offered no threat, his eyes nothing to fear, his face promised peace.
>
> [852–58]

We can see him in his splendor against the green grass. He is a fine animal, with just those characteristics that an ancient farmer would look for in a bull: a thick sinewy neck and long dewlaps. If we could think of the animal as merely a bull, the description would not, of course, be funny, but because it is really Jupiter in a bull-suit, this attention to the details of taurine perfection is comical.

Several allusions to Vergil add an additional dimension to the story for those who catch them. The description of Jupiter as bull is amusing in itself; it is even more so if we catch Ovid's allusion to Vergil's *Georgics.* In his third book Vergil makes clear that infinite pains are involved at every stage in the breeding and care of livestock and warns the farmer to choose his brood cow carefully. A good specimen must, he asserts, have long dewlaps (line 53). It is ridiculous enough for Ovid's Jupiter to be a beautiful bull; it is even more ridiculous for him to resemble a prize-winning brood cow.

Ovid concludes with the horns, normally a bull's most terrifying attribute. As is appropriate for this bull, the horns are small and therefore do not look frightening, but they are beautiful and so they are very threatening, since the danger of this bull lies in his harmless appearance. The horns, gleaming like a piece of jewelry or a sculpture ("made by hand"), take us out of the georgic world of bull necks and dewlaps into the world of the artist, creating an appropriate conclusion to Ovid's picture of a bull that is not a bull but a god in disguise, artifice and not reality, a lie (Jupiter is not a bull) that is still true (these horns are exceptionally deadly because they look harmless; Europa would probably have been safer with a real bull).

Finally, after one last summarizing sentence—no threats from his forehead, no terror from his eye, a face that offers peace—Ovid turns from the bull to Europa, who is playing with her friends. She responds to the beauty of the animal and to his seeming harmlessness:

> Europa marveled because he seemed so beautiful and unthreatening. At first she was afraid to touch him despite his mild appearance; soon she came close, however, and held out flowers to his snowy lips.
>
> [858–61]

In this wonderful description of a young girl gradually overcoming her natural fear of a dangerous animal (and also, by extension, her fear of the sexual power that this god-bull represents), Ovid depicts two stages. At first Europa is afraid to touch him, even though he looks gentle; then, drawn by his beauty, she holds out flowers for him to nibble. She sees only the externals, but Ovid shifts from Europa back to the bull and lets us into Jupiter's mind:

> The lover exulted and kissed her hands in expectation of delights to come; he could scarcely restrain himself; he

could hardly wait for the rest. And now he played up to
her and frisked about in the green grass. Now he laid his
snowy flank down on the tawny sand. And gradually
taking away her fear, he offered his breast to be patted
by her virgin hand, his horns to be entwined with new
garlands.

[862–68]

The first words stress the god: "the lover rejoiced." The next
blend god and bull: "until the hoped for pleasure might come"
is applicable to both, and "he kissed her hands" depicts the
action of both. Now the god-bull begins to show off, feeling
himself in control of the situation. The words have a double
meaning for us. They show the actions of the bull frisking in
the grass, and they describe the emotions of lecherous Jupiter
inside the bull hide. The Latin phrasing makes it clearer than
the English that his actions are all designed to get Europa on
his back. He offers his breast to be patted by a virgin hand
(in other words, *she* becomes the agent of *his* desires), and he
offers his horns to be garlanded.

Finally she takes over again as subject and makes the
move that seals her fate: she climbs up onto the bull's back:

The royal maiden also dared to sit on the bull's back, not
knowing whose back held her weight. At first the god set
his false hoof prints in the water, moving little by little
away from dry land and the sea shore, then he went
further and carried his prey over the ocean. She trembled
and looked back at the shore she had left; she held a horn
with her right hand, the other she placed on his back;
her garments trembled and billowed in the breeze.

[868–75]

Another Vergilian reminiscence adds poignancy to Europa's
decision to mount the bull. Here Ovid uses one of Vergil's

favorite adjectives, "ignorant," "unknowing," in a near-quotation of *Aeneid* 1, when Dido receives in her lap the god Cupid, thinking he is Aeneas's son, Ascanius, as Venus had plotted she should so she would fall in love with Aeneas. Vergil says, "She cuddles him, ignorant of how powerful a god was settling into her unlucky lap" [718–19]. Ovid echoes this moving moment with the changes necessary for *his* heroine, who unwittingly settles herself on the back of Jupiter, thinking him only a friendly bull. Ovid reminds us of Dido's tragedy, also set in motion by a ruthless divinity's tricking of a mortal, as his Jupiter prepares to spring his own divine trap.

Now Ovid calls Jupiter *deus*, or god, as the bull slips away with Europa—first off the beach, then among the waves by the shore, and finally galloping away with her over the sea. With the last words, "he carried his prey," Ovid—and Jupiter—throw all pretense to the winds. The word I have translated as "prey" is the word for spoil in battle and for victims of the hunt. The last lines give a beautiful, purely visual description of Europa sitting in terror as she looks back at her native land, holding a horn with her right hand, the other placed on the bull's back, her dress fluttering in the breeze. It is a portrait so vividly described that it could be painted—as indeed it has been, many times.

This is Ovid's version of the story of Europa except for the two lines that open Book 3 and dispose of her: "And already the god, having put off the false likeness of the bull, had revealed himself and was in Crete, when her father sent Cadmus to look for her" (3.1–4). And so begins the story of the house of Cadmus, Europa's brother. What Ovid has done with Europa, in fact, is to turn the preliminaries of her story into the story and leave the central action to be inferred. Ovid does not tell us what happened when Jupiter and Europa got to Crete. We know from the tradition that she was the mother, by Jupiter, of Minos and Rhadamanthus and, in some accounts, of Sarpedon, but Ovid gives no hint of this part of the story. Thus the tale of Europa illustrates one of Ovid's typical approaches to the material he uses. He never tells a story the way it has been told before—whether by Greek poets, Roman poets, or himself. He molds his material into something uniquely his own, sometimes, as here, by developing a piece of the story while leaving out what might have been the major part of it. We know what a rape scene is like—we have seen Jupiter at work before—so Ovid implies what happened with the brief phrase, "the god revealed himself."

Readers who respond to Ovid at all are unlikely to have trouble with the story of Europa, but other parts of the poem may bother them, and it is to these parts that I now turn. Why, we may ask, did Ovid choose to incorporate into the outline of Roman history in the last book of the poem a terribly long lecture by the philosopher Pythagoras? Why did he include a version of the *Aeneid* that is far less unified, and, let's face it, far less satisfying than Vergil's masterful rendering? Did he feel obliged to have an "Augustan" conclusion, even though it went against his nature, as Brooks Otis thought? Are there times when, as Rolfe Humphries says, "Ovid is bored . . . the writing becomes perfunctory—oh, well, we have to grind this part of it out, all in the day's work, and what's the difference" (p. viii)? And, since Ovid did choose to put all these very different ingredients into his mixture, what, if anything, holds it all together? I shall try to suggest some answers to these questions by looking first at the form of the poem.

When Ovid decided to write the *Metamorphoses*, there were two models he might have chosen. One was full-scale mythological epic of the Homeric and Vergilian type—long, unified narrative focusing on a limited number of heroes over a limited period of time. The other was "collective narrative"—a loose framework of discrete tales held together in large measure by the personality of the narrator. This second type was familiar to the Romans from Callimachus's *Aetia* and from Callimachus's own model, Hesiod. Also available for Ovid's consideration was a shorter form of narrative poem, often called "epyllion," or "little epic," which could be written either to stand alone or to be included in a collective narrative. Since the time of Catullus, Roman poets (under the influence of Callimachus) had tended to regard continuous epics of the Homeric type as outmoded, preferring to write either short, personal poems or "little epics." Vergil gave new life to full-scale epic when he wrote his *Aeneid*, using, on a much grander scale, the artistic principles that had been worked out for little epics by Catullus and his friends.

When Ovid decided to write a long work, he might well have chosen collective narrative as a way to avoid the dangers of writing epic in Vergil's shadow. The collective form would allow him opportunity to work with narratives of different types while staying within a genre that was approved by Roman poets and did not invite unfavorable comparison. But Ovid, being Ovid, and ever ready for a challenge, chose otherwise. He made no attempt to avoid comparison with Vergil; in fact, he went out of his way to insure that readers would compare his poem with the *Aeneid* by treating much of the same material Vergil had treated. At the same time he set out to excel Vergil. He would do what no one had ever tried to do before—he would write Homeric-Vergilian epic and Callimachean collective narrative all at once. So he tells us firmly in his introduction:

> My spirit is moved to sing of shapes changed into new bodies. Gods, inspire my undertaking (for you have changed it too), and accompany my song—finespun, continuous—from the beginning of the world to my own day.

Any Roman reader familiar with the poetry of the previous fifty years or so would recognize Ovid's proclamation of allegiance to the Callimachean principles of artistry and polish in the word I have translated as "finespun" (*deductum*). Vergil introduced the word as almost a technical term for elegant poetry on the small scale in *Eclogue* 6, in which Apollo rebukes the poet for attempting to write epic and urges him to return to pastoral:

> A shepherd, Tityrus, should feed his sheep fat, should sing his song lean (or finespun).
>
> [*Ec.* 6.4–5]

Some years earlier Catullus had expressed allegiance to the small, carefully crafted poem, as opposed to epic, with his own terminology: his introductory poem refers to its "novelty," its "polish," and its "charm," and one of the last in the collection opposes the artistry of Cinna, who spent nine years writing his *Smyrna*, an epyllion, or short epic, to the sloppy long-windedness of Hortensius, who publishes thousands of lines in a year. A Roman reader familiar with the terminology developed by Roman poets espousing Callimachean views of poetry would surely recognize Ovid's claim to be following Callimachus's terse, elegant style in the word *deductum* and his simultaneous claim to be writing epic in the word I have translated as "continuous" (*perpetuum*).

The Metamorphoses as Collective Narrative

The *Metamorphoses* contains about 250 stories that frequently run into each other so that it is hard to say exactly where one begins or ends. Sometimes a single character is featured in several different tales, but no character or set of characters is in evidence throughout the poem or even through a major portion of it. The poem seems to fall naturally into segments, from little ten- to fifteen-line episodes like that of the metamorphosis of young Cygnus into a swan (1.367–80), to long narratives like that of Phaëthon and the horses of the Sun (1.747–2.329). One of the main differences between the *Metamorphoses* and a poem like the *Aeneid* is the detachable nature of the episodes. Instead of integrating separable episodes into one unified whole, as Vergil does, for example, with Nisus and Euryalus, Ovid often seems to take special pains to emphasize the separateness of his stories. The events of the poem are set geographically all over the world: in Europe, Africa, and Asia. And although there is a basically east-west direction to the poem, with episodes set mainly in Greece in the first books, and in Italy in the last books, locations move about a great deal from story to story and even within stories. Books 3 and 4, for example, are set in the Greek city of Thebes. Much of Book 4, however, consists of tales told by characters within the story, and these tales all take place in exotic eastern localities—one in Babylon, one in Persia, and one in Lycia (southern Asia Minor). In the work as a whole, many of the stories take a character from one part of the world to another: Phaëthon's story, for example, begins in Egypt and ends in Italy. Thus the geographical setting of the poem is continually changing, but not in the orderly fashion of Aeneas's journey from Asia Minor to Italy.

The temporal setting is equally varied. Though there is a vague sense of chronological progress in the poem, which moves from the creation of the world on to the founding of Rome, and finally to Augustan Rome, Ovid seems to go out of his way to break up continuity. Take Hercules. The poem presents a number of events from Hercules' life—among them his birth, his famous "labors," and his death and apotheosis. Much of his story is told in Book 9, but he reappears in Books 12, 13, and 15. Still worse for epic continuity, even in Book 9 his story is told out of order, with his death *preceding* his birth. Similarly, when Ovid comes to tell the story of Daedalus (8.159ff.), he first tells the well-known part—how Daedalus devised wings for himself and his son, Icarus, in order to escape from Crete, how Icarus ignored his father's instructions, flew too close to the sun, and fell into the Icarian Sea. Only at the end, almost as an afterthought, does Ovid tack on an event that took place long before and that makes us completely reassess what we have just heard about Daedalus. As a young man he threw his nephew Perdix, who had been put in his care by his sister, off a wall in a jealous rage because Perdix had invented the saw and the compass. Perdix would have been killed if he had not been changed into a partridge (*perdix*) by Athena, patroness of craftsmen. We now see what we could not see before, that Icarus's death is not an accident. Daedalus is paying for his crime with his son's life, and the punishment neatly fits the crime.

These discontinuities are mild, however, compared with what Ovid does to two minor narratives in Book 2. He introduces the story of Corvus the crow with the information that his metamorphosis from white to black took place at the same time that the peacock received Argus's eyes in its tail. In other words, this story happened at the same time as an event recounted in Book 1. The chronological order of stories is: (1) Nyctimene the owl was turned into a bird as punishment for incest at some unspecified time in the past; (2) Cornix the raven escaped rape by becoming a bird; (3) Raven tattled on Aglauros and was demoted in rank below the owl; (4) Coronis cheated on Apollo (these all occurred before the narrative begins); (5) Raven meets Crow and tells Crow, who is on his way to tell on Coronis (= 4), that tattling doesn't pay (= 3); and (6) Crow tells anyway and is turned black. Ovid's order is: (1) Crow turns black at the time that Argus's eyes were installed in the peacock's tail (that is, in the past); (2) Coronis commits adultery and a bird goes to tell Apollo; (3) Crow meets Raven, Raven advises Crow not to tell; (4) Raven tells the story of Aglauros, proving that tattling doesn't pay because she was punished for it herself by being demoted below Owl, who had been metamorphosed for incest (= past relative to 1, 2, 3, and 4); (5) Raven tells the story of her metamorphosis into a bird (past relative to 4); and (6) Crow tells on Coronis and turns black. One's head is spinning by the time one gets this all figured out. Clearly Ovid did not (at least, not always) want his poem to move neatly in one direction from the beginning of time to his own day.

Ovid's poem has, further, many too many major characters for continuity. In its pages we find all the gods of the pantheon as well as scores of minor divinities—nymphs, fauns, river gods, and the like. Nearly every hero anyone has ever heard of has his story told somewhere in the poem, whether he is associated with the fall of Troy, the story of Thebes, or one of the great adventure tales—the journey of the Argo, the exploits of Theseus, and so on. And then there are the mortals—powerful kings and poor peasants, sinners and saints, men, women, and children from all nations, as well as a variety of animals, domestic and wild. Their stories take many different forms. Nearly every genre of poetry known to the Romans is represented somewhere in the poem. There are epic or heroic sections: the adventures of Perseus in Books 4 and 5, the Calydonian boar hunt in 8, the battle of Lapiths and Centaurs in 12, Ovid's "Aeneid" in 13 and 14. The speech of the philosopher Pythagoras in 15 is a long example of didactic poetry. Myrrha's monologue in 10 would be at home in tragedy. Byblis (Book 9) sends a poetic epistle quite like one of Ovid's *Heroides*. There are pastoral sections, elegiac sections, hymns, and so on. The poem has fittingly been called a "fifteen book exercise in mixed genre" (John Fyler, "Omnia Vincit Amor," *Classical Journal* 66 [1971]: 197).

No ancient epic has such varied subject matter as the *Metamorphoses*. It has tales about love and hate, about piety and impiety, about divine vengeance, divine justice, and divine malevolence. It has comedies, it has tragedies, and it covers the subject matter of the *Iliad* and the *Odyssey* as well as the *Aeneid*. It has scientific sections and philosophical and historical sections, and it touches on most of Greek mythology and much of Roman legend. This sort of variety is not surprising in a collective poem; it is quite extraordinary in a poem also purporting to be epic.

Also unusual in epic is Ovid's tendency, when linking one story to another, to use a transition that masks the inherent connection between the two. One of his favorite ways of ending a story is to introduce a gathering of people from which only one person is absent, launching into the new tale to explain why the person is missing. Thus he ends Daphne's tale with a gathering of river gods who wonder whether to congratulate or condole with Peneus on his daughter's metamorphosis into a laurel tree, concluding: "Only the river Inachus was absent and, hidden in his inmost cavern, he increased his waters with his tears and wretchedly lamented his daughter Io, as lost" (1.583–85). This is a clever, but hardly a "significant," transition from Daphne to Io. It does not encourage us to see the striking similarities between the two stories.

A number of things, then, seem calculated to pull Ovid's poem apart, among them his use of place and time, his variety of characters and types of stories, and his "weak" links between individual sections. Yet it is clear that he has taken pains to link the parts of his poem together as well. An elaborate structure of cross references reminds us of what is past and points us toward what is to come. It is true that the poem is so long and full of characters and events that readers reading for pleasure will not pick up on all the allusions to what has preceded. But there are enough verbal and thematic echoes back and forth, enough reappearances of characters and situations we have seen before, that we are bound to recognize some of them as old friends when they emerge again.

Certainly no one can miss the similarity of situation of the rape victims in the first books. Daphne's story initiates a series of such tales: the attempted rape of Daphne by Apollo, the rape of Io by Jupiter, the attempted rape of Syrinx by Pan, and the rape of Callisto by Jupiter. The basic situation is that a mortal girl becomes the object of a male god's lust. Within this situation, Daphne belongs to one type of victim, a type I like to call "militant virgins." A follower of Diana, hostile to men and marriage, she is pursued by a loving Apollo and rescued from him in the nick of time by being turned into a laurel. In the next story in the sequence, Ovid varies the victim type. Io is not a devotee of Diana like Daphne, though her fate is worse than Daphne's. Not only is she raped by Jupiter, but she is hounded by a vengeful Juno—a new motif in the basic story. With the story of Syrinx Ovid returns to the militant virgin theme but changes the effect of the story utterly by beginning it as a story used as a weapon (tell a boring story so your listener will fall asleep and you can cut his head off) and ending by telling it as a nonstory (for which see pp. 135ff.): what Mercury would have told Argus if Argus had not fallen asleep. Syrinx's story prepares the way for Callisto, who is the culmination of the militant virgin type; she is actually one of Diana's band. Her fate is to be brutally raped by Jupiter (like Io), punished for her loss of virginity by Diana, and then punished again (also like Io) by Juno, who turns her into a bear. Finally, after nearly being killed by her own son, she is turned into a constellation by Jupiter, a dubious honor undercut again by Juno, who arranges that the Bear will not, like other constellations, bathe in Ocean.

Having rung the changes on the theme of the threatened or ravished virgin, in the last episode Ovid introduces a new theme—human misconduct toward the gods—which he will take up in the next series of stories. Only hinted at in Callisto's story, this theme culminates in the weaving contest between Arachne and Minerva and the tale of Niobe. The tale of Arachne, in turn, proves to be the first major story in a sequence about the failure of artists that culminates with Orpheus in Book 10. In this way, then, through the evolution of character types, Ovid links whole sections of the poem.

Similar efforts to achieve thematic continuity may be seen in Ovid's handling of the house of Cadmus in Books 3 and 4. He does not follow earlier writers, who tell the stories generation by generation: first what happened to the children of Cadmus and Harmonia (Semele, the mother of Bacchus, Autonoe, the mother of Actaeon, Agave, the mother of Pentheus, and Ino, the mother of Melicertes and Learchus), then what happened to the various grandchildren. Instead, he begins with the story of Diana's vengeance on the innocent Actaeon, one of the grandchildren, and only then goes on to the story of Semele, Actaeon's aunt. Actaeon is a hunter who accidentally stumbles on Diana bathing and sees the nakedness no man is allowed to see. He is punished for this crime by being turned into a deer and set upon by his own hunting dogs. Despite his innocence he is punished as a criminal. (Ovid uses Actaeon as an emblem for himself in *Tr.* 2.105ff.) This story establishes a pattern of divine cruelty that is taken up next in the tale of Semele. Juno detests the line of Cadmus because Cadmus is the brother of Europa, another of Jupiter's victims, as we have seen. She is thus delighted at what has happened to Actaeon and is spurred to punish Semele, another female of the hated line and another of Jupiter's mistresses. Using Diana's punishment of Actaeon as a model,

Juno goes after Semele, who is pregnant with Bacchus. She destroys the mother but misses the son, who is rescued by Jupiter. Bacchus then punishes Pentheus, his cousin, for his refusal to accept Bacchus's divinity, and Pentheus is dismembered by his own mother and aunt, much as Actaeon was torn apart by his own dogs. In the final, and most terrible, episode of the group, Juno imitates Bacchus's punishment of the guilty Pentheus, this time going after the last member of the Theban line and destroying not only Ino and Athamas but their children also. As Brooks Otis says, "Ovid's arrangement of the Theban stories . . . has a dramatic logic that quite surpasses the logic of genealogy" (p. 131).

Despite discontinuities, then, a number of links hold parts of the poem together. What, if anything, holds the poem as a whole together? One answer is the transparent presence *in* the poem of an "Ovid," who talks to his characters and his readers and is very much a part of the stories he tells (not unlike the narrator in Byron's *Don Juan*). We seldom forget that we are listening to tales by a master storyteller who obtrudes his presence on his story, creating an ever-changing relationship between myth, poet, and audience. To this extent we can see the *Metamorphoses* as a natural conclusion to the development Ovid began with the *Amores* and continued in the *Heroides* and *Ars*.

Ovid's discontinuous style, his parentheses, asides, puns, incongruities of style and content—all are designed to keep the narrator's voice and personality in the foreground. He seems to pop his head in and out of his narrative to tell us how we are to take it. For instance, in Book 1, Jupiter rapes Io and then, aware that Juno is on the way, turns the girl into a cow. Juno, ever suspicious of her philandering husband, asks for the cow as a present. Ovid begins inside Jupiter's head and runs through the alternatives:

What is he to do? It would be cruel to hand over his love;
not to give her would create suspicion.

[617–18]

Then the poet separates himself from Jupiter and becomes
commentator, lest we miss the issues:

It is Shame that persuades the one course, Love that dis-
suades.

[618–19]

Shame wins out, but only because otherwise a cow might
seem not to be a cow, after all:

Shame would have been conquered by Love, but if the
trifling gift of a cow were to be refused his sister and
bedmate, it might seem not to be a cow.

[619–21]

In the last two lines narrator Ovid merges again with the
adulterer and the affair dissolves itself in a grin.

When he tells Callisto's story (2.417ff.), Ovid makes sim-
ilar quick changes in aesthetic distance, with comic results.
He begins with a cool outsider's narrative and moves on to a
degree of engagement when he wishes that Juno were watch-
ing—she would know that Callisto did all a girl could to resist,
but "how could a mere girl defeat Jupiter?" (436–37). Next
comes impassioned partisanship, as narrator merges with vic-
tim, and in the phrase, "alas, how difficult it is not to betray
the crime through facial expression" (447), we cannot be sure
whose voice we hear. Then, with a final wink, Ovid separates
himself from his character and allies himself with the reader,
smiling in kindly but superior fashion at the naïveté of Diana,
who, being a virgin, is too ignorant of the world to realize
what has happened to Callisto:

And if she hadn't been a virgin, Diana could have real-
ized her guilt by a thousand signs.

[2.451–52]

Elsewhere Ovid comically pits reader against narrator, giving
us with avuncular condescension the information he seems
to think we need. "Don't run away from me," says Jupiter to
Io (1.597), in a speech which Ovid soberly interrupts for our
benefit: ("for she was running away"). The aside is funny, but
it also draws attention to itself and thus to the mind of its
creator. In this way, throughout the *Metamorphoses*, Ovid's
narrator manages to keep in close touch. One finds oneself
talking to him, reacting to him. With his regular tendency to
see the "laughter in things" as well as the "tears in things"
that Vergil saw, the sparkling play of his personality performs
a unifying that even some of its most disparate elements can-
not entirely destroy.

So far we have been looking at the poem as an example
of collective narrative: episodic, fragmented, infinitely varied,
but nevertheless tied together by an omnipresent golden
thread. We have yet to see anything other than Ovid's phrase
"continuous song" in 1.4 to justify calling it an epic.

The Metamorphoses as an Epic

In spite of its lack of many of the characteristics we as-
sociate with epic—a major hero, a unified plot with temporal
and geographical centering, careful integration of episodes
into a single whole—Ovid clearly viewed his poem as a kind
of epic. All his surviving poems are written in elegiac couplets
except for the *Metamorphoses*, which is in dactylic hexameter,
the epic meter. (For the differences between the two, see the
Metrical Appendix.) It can hardly be without significance that
Ovid chose to write his one long, more or less continuous

poem in that meter, whereas the *Fasti*, in part similar in sub-
ject matter, is in elegiac couplets. The language of the *Meta-
morphoses* is likewise similar to Vergil's language in the *Aeneid*.
Extended comparisons, or similes, in which the poet describes
a person, scene, or situation in terms of something outside
his text (warriors compared to wolves, for example), are a
commonplace of epic, and Ovid's poem contains even more
of them than Vergil's. (Similes are not, of course, limited to
epic, but they are a distinctive feature of it, and many of
Ovid's similes follow patterns set for epic similes by previous
poets.)

Certain epic themes had also become traditional by
Ovid's time. Among these are the heroic feast at which a long
narrative is presented as entertainment and the "council of
the gods" at which gods debate human affairs. Ovid has both.
Battles between heroes are, of course, a standard feature of
epic, taking place mostly on the battlefield but occasionally
indoors, and again Ovid sprinkles such battles through his
poem (in Books 5, 8, 9, 12, 13, and 14). He includes also
another traditional epic feature, the journey. When heroes are
not fighting they are usually voyaging. Ovid's Perseus circles
the world, his Ulysses makes his way gradually homeward,
and his Aeneas follows in the footsteps of Vergil's Aeneas as
he sets out from Troy to found an empire.

In fact, much in the *Metamorphoses* becomes clearer if we
see Ovid's poem not only as an epic but specifically as an
answer to Vergil's *Aeneid*, defining itself and guiding our re-
sponses by reference to Vergil's poem, just as Pope's *Essay on
Man* establishes what it is and is not by reference to Lucretius
and Milton. The *Metamorphoses* contains most of the subject
matter of the *Aeneid*, in one way or other. It is crammed with
quotations from the *Aeneid* from beginning to end. Sometimes
Ovid quotes Vergil with a correction, as when his Juno, jeal-
ous that Semele is pregnant with Jupiter's child, cites Vergil's

angry Juno of *Aeneid* 1. Vergil's Juno, furious that she has had so little success hounding the Trojans, describes herself impressively as "queen and at once sister and wife of Jupiter" (46–47), to contrast the dignity of her position with her ineffectiveness. Ovid's Juno remembers the comment she made in the other poem and modifies it, saying, "if I am queen and at once sister and wife of Jupiter—sister, at any rate" (3.265–66). The comment is funny in itself, expressing the frustration of the wife of a husband with an ever-roving eye; it is funnier still if we catch the Vergilian echo. But it is more than funny. It suggests an altogether different conception of the gods, and this fits into Ovid's different conception of epic. Ovid drains the majesty from the Olympians.

We can see this on a larger scale in Ovid's version of the council of the gods, again based on Vergil's:

> Meanwhile the house of all-powerful Olympus opened and the father of gods and king of men called a council to his starry abode whence he looked down from on high, on all lands and the Trojan camp and Latin peoples. They sat down in his double-doored house and he began.
>
> [*Aen.* 10.1–5]

> As soon as the Saturnian father saw these things from his lofty citadel, he groaned, and recalling the disgusting feast of Lycaon's table, not yet public knowledge because so recent a deed, he conceived in his heart a wrath so enormous and worthy to be the wrath of Jupiter, and called a council. No one who was called delayed.
>
> [*Meta.* 1.163–67]

Vergil creates a splendid setting suitable to the god he calls "father of gods and king of men" whose realm is located high among the stars, physically and spiritually distant from earth and human affairs. His Jupiter looks down impartially on Latin and Trojan, the hostile forces linked in his god's eye view. Ovid too creates a setting suitable for the greatest of the immortals. But what a difference! Ovid's Jupiter looks down from a fortress, very like a human potentate. He does not view impartially but reacts to events on earth. Something has just happened, so recent it has not yet been publicized, something awful connected with Lycaon's table. As a result he is furious and has summoned the gods, who rush to his side. The portrait that begins to emerge here depicts a society that is all too like human society: a self-important and self-righteous king with a first-rate intelligence service that reports only to him and underlings who are afraid to disobey him (why else do they rush to answer his call?)

The next paragraph is a fanciful addition of Ovid's, inserted to fill out this mocking portrait:

> There is a road on high, conspicuous in a clear sky; it is called "milky," famous for its brightness. This is the route the gods take to the palace, the royal abode of the great Thunderer. On right and left the halls of the noble gods are thronged, doors open. The plebs lives elsewhere; here the powerful and illustrious denizens of the sky have established their household gods. This is the place which, if I may be so bold, I should hardly be afraid to call the Palatine of the great heavens.
>
> [1.168–76]

The Milky Way is the road to Jupiter's palace, and it is also the better part of town, the right side of the tracks in the sky, where the aristocrats live. Ordinary citizen gods live off somewhere else—in public housing, one supposes—somewhere not worth naming. Enough said of them! A further touch, which no one but Ovid would have included in an epic context, completes this comic sketch of divine society. Ovid finally makes explicit the equation he has been suggesting between the divine and the human by venturing the opinion, comically wondering at his own audacity, that this is the Palatine (the fashionable dwelling area of Rome) of the sky. Vergil's passage has been made the starting point of something wholly Ovidian.

Here, and throughout, Ovid shows that he can use Vergilian material to question the sense of historical purpose and direction that Vergil had imposed on Roman history, and by this means, indeed, to question the whole notion of heroism central to epic.

Ovid's Treatment of the Heroic

One of the many strands in Ovid's massive tapestry is "the heroic." It will be useful to separate this strand out from the others in order to look at it, even though Ovid very carefully wove it in. The first full-scale heroic episode is the "Perseid" (4.614ff.). Perseus is introduced to us (*after* he has performed his most famous deed, his beheading of the Gorgon Medusa) flying through the air while blood drips from the Gorgon's head. He flies around the world three times, landing at dusk because, Ovid tells us soberly, he is afraid to fly at night—a sensible man, Perseus, flying before the invention of radar, but what kind of hero can we expect if he is so timid about night flying? Landing in the territory of King Atlas, he demands overnight shelter on the basis of his important family connections and his deeds:

"Friend," said Perseus to him, "if you are impressed by the greatness of the glory of one's family, Jupiter is the author of my birth; but if you are an admirer of deeds, you will certainly admire mine."

Epic heroes have never been known for their modesty—many a student has balked at Vergil's "I am pious Aeneas, and my glory reaches beyond the skies" (*Aen.* 1.378–79)—but Perseus's self-congratulation seems excessive. Atlas, unimpressed, decides to fight. Perseus wins, even though he is weaker than Atlas, by turning him to stone. So much for our hero's first heroic adventure—a fight won by guile.

When the sun comes up, Perseus resumes his wings, goes back to flying, and spies Andromeda tied to a cliff—a truly heroic adventure in the making. The narrator begins in typical objective fashion:

> As soon as Perseus saw her, her arms bound to the hard rock, he . . .

[672–73]

then moves into Perseus's head with a startling contrary-to-fact statement of what Perseus would have thought:

> Except for the fact that a light breeze had stirred her hair and that her eyes were wet with warm tears, he would have thought her a marble statue.

[673–75]

There is something strange about this parenthesis. It intrudes on the narrative by making us think about the narrator who has turned what might have been an epic simile (just as a marble statue . . . so Andromeda . . .) into what might have been a thought in the hero's mind. (Perhaps also it reminds us of the Gorgon's head, with which Perseus will shortly create many marble statues.) Perseus's response to this spectacle is to fall in love at first sight. He is so struck by the beauty of his beloved that he almost forgets to flap his wings—a detail that not only allows us a comic glimpse of lovesick admirer hovering over bound girl but invites us to speculate momentarily on what would have happened if he had indeed forgotten: a fall like Icarus's into the sea. When Perseus speaks, the comedy builds:

"O," he said, "lady-not-worthy-of-those-chains-but-of-those-which-bind-eager-lovers-together, reveal, for one who wants to know, your name and that of your country and why you wear chains."

[678–81]

The long periphrasis with its implied compliment, standing at the point where in ordinary Latin discourse we expect a personal name, the placement of "he said" coming after "O" and interrupting the elaborate title before it gets underway, the Homeric motif in reverse (for it is usually the newcomer who is asked to identify himself), the fetters treated as if they were bracelets, the sense of formality and leisure appropriate to a drawing room—all of these are so out of place under the circumstances that we can hardly avoid laughter.

Now Andromeda has her turn. The narrator takes up a post inside her head, telling us what she does and what she would have done if she had been able:

At first she is silent. She doesn't dare, she a virgin, to address a man, and would have modestly covered her face with her hands, if she hadn't been tied up.

[681–83]

Again, all this maidenly modesty, while perhaps appropriate to a drawing room, is ridiculous in a maiden tied to a rock and about to be devoured by a monster. Once she gets over her initial shyness, moreover, she is quite happy to tell Perseus at some length who she is, where she is from, and why she is chained to the rock, laying the blame where it belongs, squarely on her mother. The arrival of the sea monster interrupts this chat:

The girl shrieks; the unhappy father and mother are at her side, both in misery, she more justly so, and they bring not help but tears and lamentation, suited to the occasion, and cling to the girl's chained body.

[691–94]

The time is ripe for the hero to act. He does so, but only after a speech telling the parents that there is not time to weep (1½ lines), proclaiming his lineage and exploits (4 lines), and making a bargain with the parents for the girl (3 lines). As the narrator says, "they accept his terms (for who would hesitate?) and, in addition, promise him a kingdom as dowry" (704–5). Now for the epic action. If one epic simile is good, Ovid implies, four must be better, and they come thick and fast. In fact, there is almost as much simile as there is narrative. At last, when the battle and the similes are over, Perseus washes his hands (a nice homey touch), setting the Gorgon's head on the ground, where it turns all the twigs into coral. Why should Ovid at this moment choose to mention the head? Possibly to remind us that Perseus was never in any danger at all, that the great contest was, in fact, a farce, since Perseus had his ace in the hole all the time.

At the wedding feast of Perseus and Andromeda that follows, Perseus, like Odysseus in the *Odyssey* and Aeneas in the *Aeneid*, is asked to tell his story (772–89). Surprisingly, he speaks briefly (18 lines versus Odysseus's 2180 and Aeneas's 1517). Furthermore, against all epic convention, his words are not quoted directly but reported by the narrator: "the hero tells that. . . ." In this account, too, the deed itself is seen to be unheroic. Only craft and stealth, not valor, were needed. In fact, the first part of the story is told so obliquely that it would be difficult to figure out what happened if one did not know. According to other versions, Perseus stole the one eye that the Graiae, sisters of the Gorgons, shared, forcing them to tell where the Gorgons were or, alternatively, preventing them in their blindness from helping their sisters. Ovid's version gives no hint of a connection between Graiae and Gorgons. Perseus merely stole the eye as it was passed around and went along to the Gorgons' home, where he cut off Medusa's head while both she and her snakes were asleep. Simple as that! So we have what ought to be but is not a heroic action, recounted in a startlingly unheroic way that is also unepically brief: "Perseus fell silent before they expected" (790).

One further detail may be a part of the mockery. The narrator specifies that the dangers Perseus told of his homeward journey were "not false" (787)—a statement calculated perhaps to make us wonder. I will return to the question of a narrator's credibility later on. For now it is enough to see that Ovid may well be introducing yet another unepic notion into a seemingly epic situation. When we read the *Odyssey,* we accept Odysseus's account of his adventures (in Books 9– 12) as what probably actually happened, although we know from elsewhere that Odysseus is a good liar, just as we accept Homer's narration as the poetic truth. Similarly, when we listen to Aeneas's account of his trials in Books 2 and 3, it never crosses our minds that he might be exaggerating to win Dido's sympathy, even though we are constantly aware from his comments that he is telling of things long ago. When Ovid does, at last, give us the first-person speech that epic conventions lead us to expect, it turns out to concern something Perseus knows only by hearsay—how Medusa got her snaky hair: "I found someone who *said he had seen* her. Neptune *is said* to have raped her" (797–99).

Since every epic needs an epic fray, Book 5 supplies one. Ovid combines elements from Odysseus's slaughter of the suitors in *Odyssey* 22 with the battles of the second half of the *Aeneid* to create his own mock-epic scene. The characters are modeled on those from the *Aeneid.* Perseus arrives in Ethiopia, and, with the approval of her father, King Cepheus, wins the princess Andromeda away from her fiancé, Phineus. Similarly, Aeneas arrives in Italy and, with the approval of her father, King Latinus, wins the princess Lavinia away from Turnus, to whom she was, at least in his view and in that of her mother, betrothed. Unlike the characters of the *Aeneid*, however, Ovid's possess no ennobling virtues. Phineus is a coward; Perseus is not much of a hero either and when the going gets rough simply takes out his trusty Gorgon's head and petrifies the last two hundred of the enemy. The ending is splendidly unheroic. When Phineus begs Perseus for mercy, renouncing his claim to Andromeda, Perseus responds:

> What I can give—and it is a great gift for a coward—I will grant, put away your fear. You will not be violated by the sword. Rather, I shall make a memorial of you to last through time—to be on view in my father-in-law's house so that my wife can take solace in the image of her fiancé.
>
> [5.224–29]

This domestic touch is the final blow to the heroic. Death in battle is expected in epic, and all the epic poets linger over descriptions of death and sometimes over the memorials that will keep the hero's name alive to future ages. But this is outrageous. Phineus, no hero to begin with, destroyed not by his opponent's prowess but by a magic trick, will serve as his own burlesque memorial as well as Ovid's burlesque memorial of the epic theme:

> in marble the cowardly face and suppliant look, the submissive hands and cringing expression remained.
>
> [234–35]

Everywhere the strategy of the *Metamorphoses* is to take the heroism out of the heroic while professing to write in the heroic mode. The Calydonian boar hunt, Ovid's "Aeneid," and Nestor's story of the Lapiths and Centaurs are all cases in point. In the boar-hunt episode (8.267ff.), the great heroes of the pre-Homeric generation are made to behave like characters in a slapstick farce. Nestor runs away from the boar and vaults into a nearby tree, using his spear as the pole (and thus, presumably, inventing the pole vault). Telamon trips over a root and falls on his face. The great warrior Jason levels his javelin at the boar and hits an innocent hunting dog. Ancaeus, enraged because Atalanta, the token woman in the hunt, has grazed the boar, brags (with surely sexual overtones?): "learn from me how a man's weapons outclass a woman's," and gets a tusk in the groin. Finally, when Meleager kills the boar and all crowd round to admire the beast, they are afraid at first to touch it.

Ovid's most extensive treatment of the "heroic," making up nearly a fifth of his poem, is his account in Books 12–14 of the Trojan War and its aftermath in his versions of the *Iliad*, the *Odyssey*, and the *Aeneid*. These little epics have often been considered failures, especially the "Aeneid," which seems to be an attempt to deal with the whole of Vergil's story. Read as an attempt to do what Vergil did, it *is* a failure—it falls apart, it has no direction and no thematic unity. Sometimes it reads as a plot summary of the *Aeneid* (lines 78–81 represent the first four books of Vergil's poem), sometimes it spins out something that was of little or no significance in the *Aeneid* (few of us even wondered whether Anius in *Aeneid* 5 had any children—well, he did, Ovid tells us). Ovid's "Aeneid" contains a number of chunks of the *Odyssey* as well. Everywhere Ovid's emphasis is different from Vergil's, and his non-Vergilian material is much more interesting than his Vergilian material. Is Ovid's "Aeneid" a failure, then? I think it is part of a brilliant parody of the whole idea of the heroic. Homer's view of life is only one way of viewing life, Ovid's poem seems to say, offering us another. Vergil's notion of the shape

and direction of history, moving inexorably—for better or
worse—toward Augustan Rome is only one way, Ovid sug-
gests, of viewing that history. And so he incorporates Roman
history in a framework of Greek myth and makes Vergil's
Aeneid only a fragment in a much larger whole. He does not
try to vie with Vergil in his telling of the story of Aeneas but
turns it into a vehicle for his own imaginative elaborations.
As Aeneas trudges gloomily ever onward toward Rome, Ovid
carries his readers into other worlds where sea nymphs comb
each other's hair and tell stories of their love affairs so en-
chantingly that we come to regret the inevitable return to
Aeneas. It should not surprise us that Ovid has his Pytha-
goras both predict the eminence of Augustan Rome and list
it with the other great civilizations that have flourished and
disappeared (15.426ff.). Eternal Rome was never Ovid's
dream. Change conquers all.

As we turn to Nestor we should keep in mind that Nes-
tor's account of the battle between the Lapiths and Centaurs
stands, essentially, for Homer's *Iliad*. Ovid's "Iliad" is reduced
from Homer's twenty-four books to a brief account of a battle
between Achilles and Cygnus, the Hector of Ovid's "Iliad"
(12.64–124), and a long story told by Nestor about the glorious
past (12.169–576). Nestor's eyewitness account of the battle of
the Lapiths and Centaurs parodies that moment in the epic
scheme of things when a bard sings of heroic action for the
entertainment of warriors at a feast. Ovid's Nestor is quite
similar to Homer's Nestor. He is very old, he loves to talk,
and he generally tells long stories about the past. But we do
not sneer at Homer's Nestor, even if we smile at him. He
possesses the wisdom as well as the foibles of old age, and
his younger colleagues listen to him with respect.

Ovid sets the scene for *his* Nestor in the first part of
Book 12 and then steps aside and lets the old man speak for
himself. The banquet takes place during a truce in the Trojan

War. Present are Nestor, Achilles, Tlepolemus, and other Greeks who are not named. Ovid establishes our attitude, as he so often does, by alluding to the *Aeneid*. Book 1 in that epic ends with a song about the nature of things sung by the bard Iopas, followed by Dido's desire to protract the evening with Aeneas by persuading him to tell of his adventures:

> And unhappy Dido drew out the night in varied conversation drinking deep of her love.
>
> [*Aen*. 1.748–49]

Ovid embeds part of Vergil's line 748 in his line 159 to finish off his description of the banqueting Greeks and to indicate that we should compare this feasting scene with that:

> *they* do not want the lyre nor unaccompanied singing; *they* do not want the long box-wood flute; they draw out the night with conversation, and prowess is the subject of their talk.
>
> [*Meta*. 12.157–60]

Vergil's banqueters, the implication is, enjoyed music and song; Ovid's Greeks, in contrast, have no taste for culture: they do not want to listen to a song about the nature of the universe like that at the end of *Aeneid* 1, nor do they want to listen to heroic song like that of Aeneas. What they want to do is to talk—about themselves, of course. Nestor replaces the traditional bard, talk replaces song. "Virtue" or "courage" is to be their topic. The irony in their choice of word emerges gradually as we search in vain for any indications of valor in the gory account of slaughter that follows.

Ovid's characterization of Nestor continues with Achilles' address to the old man, "O eloquent old man, wisdom of our age" (12.178). Once again the full irony of this is only gradually revealed. Homer's Nestor might well be described in this way. Ovid's Nestor is never at a loss for words, but if he

is "the wisdom of our age," the age is in trouble. The story
he is about to relate, he says, is the most memorable of all
the things he has experienced in his two hundred years and
must, one would therefore think, be important. And since, in
spite of his advanced age and occasional lapses of memory,
it remains vividly fixed in his mind, his account of it is surely
to be trusted. We are in for a shock on both counts. We find
as the tale proceeds that the old man has an extraordinary
memory for trifles. He remembers not only what weapons
were made of but the direction they came from and which
side of the body they hit. Seeming to think that his audience
is as obsessed with clinical detail as he is, he even apologizes
for not remembering what wounds five of the centaurs died
of: "I don't remember the wounds, I noted the name and the
number" (12.461). In spite of this disclaimer, wounds are
what interest him most. One centaur vomits gobs of blood
and a mixture of brains and wine from his mouth and a
wound; another's eyes are gouged by stag antlers, and a mix-
ture of blood and eyeball runs down his beard; a Lapith's
eyes are popped from their sockets as his nose is bashed
down his throat; a centaur's entrails get tangled around his
legs and trip him up. Such details do not lead us to ponder
the tragedy of warfare; they are too many and too gruesome.
They serve only to make us shudder or to defend ourselves
by smiling. How can we take seriously a man who not only
remembers but relishes this brutality? And how can we take
seriously a society that entertains itself with such violence at
the banquet table?

Reliability

After Nestor finishes his long, tedious tale, one of his
listeners, Hercules' son, Tlepolemus, asks why Hercules was
not mentioned, saying that his father had often told him about

his victories over Centaurs. The implication is, even though it apparently is not true, that Hercules did fight in that very battle and that Nestor left him out of his account of it. Nestor admits to his good friend that Hercules did indeed perform heroic feats (and again he *sounds* as if he is admitting that Hercules did fight in the battle) but that he said nothing about him because he was angry at Hercules, who had killed Nestor's brothers and destroyed his home. In other words, Nestor would have left Hercules out of his account of the battle if Hercules had, in fact, been present, no matter what feats he might have performed. A story is what its narrator makes it. Hercules' version of that battle would have been different and might equally have excluded Nestor. It is a fine stroke of Ovid's to let the old man tell his story so graphically and then undercut him with the hint that a totally different "truth" could exist.

Nowhere else in the *Metamorphoses* does Ovid pull the rug out from under a narrator so completely as he does here, but he frequently makes it clear that a given story has other possible versions. The Cephalus and Procris story (7.672–862), as Brooks Otis points out (pp. 176ff.), contains undercurrents of a different, and much more sordid, story that Cephalus is suppressing as he tells the Myrmidons what happened to his wife, Procris. According to Cephalus, he loved his wife but spent a great deal of time away from her to hunt. One day he was accosted by Aurora, goddess of the dawn, who tried to seduce him while he was resting from the hunt. When he rebuffed her she planted the seeds of suspicion in him about his wife's virtue: "keep Procris . . . but if my mind sees the future, you will wish you had not" (7.12–13). Suspicious that Procris had been unfaithful in his absence, he went home in disguise to spy on her and test her loyalty, but she was firm in rejecting his advances. Finally he admitted that he was Cephalus. Procris was furious and went

off to the mountains to live the celibate life of Diana and her
followers. But after Cephalus admitted that he himself might
have yielded, if someone had wooed him as ardently as he,
in his disguise, had wooed her, she forgave him and returned
home, presenting him with a wonderful dog and a spear. The
two lived happily together, but Cephalus returned to his
hunting, and was overheard addressing the breeze Aura in
such a way that it sounded as if he were addressing a woman;
"you are my great joy," he would say, and "you refresh me
and warm me." Procris, having been informed that her hus-
band was in love with a nymph named Aura, went out to
investigate. Cephalus, hearing something rustle in the
bushes, hurled his spear and hit and killed his wife. As we
read this story we can see that it consists of three strands.
The first two, the story of past events (what happened to
Cephalus and Procris) and old Cephalus's reaction to the
events that happened to young Cephalus, give us the same
kind of interaction of narrator with narrative that we find in
Books 2 and 3 of the *Aeneid*, in which Aeneas tells Dido the
story of the fall of Troy and of his wanderings. But Ovid hints
at a third level by comments that do not make sense in terms
of the account Cephalus tells but that fit a less innocent ver-
sion. In a version of the tale found in Pherecydes (fifth century
B.C.), Cephalus, in order to test his new wife, leaves her, still
a virgin, saying he is going to travel for eight years. (This
might explain Ovid's otherwise enigmatic references to Pro-
cris's unhappiness at her husband's hunting absences at the
beginning of his version of the story—she is said to be "sad,"
her husband is said to have been "snatched away" from her.)
In Pherecydes, Procris yields to the apparent stranger (her
husband in disguise) who tries to seduce her. She is im-
pressed by his promised present, a gold necklace, and by his
good looks. If this story, or one like it, lurks behind Ovid's
version, a number of oddities become clear. When Ovid's Ce-
phalus begs Procris's pardon for having tested her, he says:

and I confessed that I had sinned and that I could have
given in to a similar fault if I had been given so many
presents.

[7.748–50]

The wording implies that Procris *did* give in. And she:

having first avenged her injured modesty, came back to
me and spent delightful years in harmony.

[751–52]

This reference to avenging injured modesty certainly has the
ring of something Cephalus is suppressing. In the version
found in Apollodorus's *Library* (summaries of Greek myths,
written probably in the first or second century A.D.), Procris
is seduced by Pteleon (with a gold crown as a bribe), and
when Cephalus finds out she flees to Crete. There she is se-
duced by King Minos (with the dog and the spear as a bribe).
Copulation with Minos was normally fatal because his wife,
Pasiphae, had punished him for his many infidelities by caus-
ing him to ejaculate snakes, but Procris protects herself by
concocting a prophylactic potion for the king. Afterwards she
returns to Athens with the dog and the spear. No innocent
wife is this Procris! Finally, in the story as told in Hyginus's
Fabulae (a handbook of mythology compiled from Greek
sources, probably in the second century A.D.), Procris gets
her own back for Cephalus's seduction of her when he was
in disguise: she masquerades as a boy and seduces him in
her turn—he is eager to buy the dog and the spear but she
refuses to sell, even when he promises part of his kingdom.
She says she will give in only if he promises to give "what
boys customarily give," and Cephalus, so desperate to gain
the dog and the spear, agrees to an apparently homosexual
affair with his own wife. All of this is a far cry from anything
Ovid's Cephalus says outright, but again, something like this
is needed to explain his reference to Procris's revenge and

the gifts that could have seduced him. A careful reader may
see traces of these other versions of the story in the version
Cephalus actually tells.

Sometimes the narrator is so biased that we cannot be
sure what the story really is, as in the contest between the
Muses and the Pierides in 5.300ff. Minerva goes to Mount
Helicon to visit the Muses and to see the spring created by
Pegasus. While she is there, a group of magpies settle in a
tree and begin chattering in a very human-sounding way. In
explanation, a Muse tells a story in which the Pierides chal-
lenge the Muses' right to be goddesses of poetry, the nymphs
act as judges of the ensuing singing contest, and the Pierides
are punished for their overweening pride by being trans-
formed into magpies. The Muse, however, allows us the bar-
est sketch of the quality of the Pierides' song:

> She sings the wars of the gods above and falsely honors
> the giants and belittles the deeds of the great gods, telling
> how Typhoeus, let loose from the depths of the earth,
> terrified the Olympians and put them all to flight until
> Egypt and the seven-mouthed Nile received the tired
> gods. She says that earth-born Typhoeus came here too
> and that the gods concealed themselves in lying shapes—
> Jupiter became a ram, leader of the flock, which is why
> Jupiter Ammon is now portrayed with curved horns.
> Apollo became a raven, Dionysus a goat, Diana a cat,
> Juno a snow-white cow, Venus lurks in a fish, Mercury
> is a winged ibis.
>
> [5.319–31]

The Muse insists that the Pierides' song was a poor effort
(blasphemous it certainly was!), but she does not give us
enough information to judge anything but its subject matter.
The song as she sketches it is 13 lines long, only 5 of which
are quoted directly, and those 5 are only the bare list of the

gods in their animal disguises. Calliope's song about Ceres and Proserpina, the winning entry in the contest, on the other hand, is 320 lines long, all in direct quotation. Since the attitude toward the gods expressed by the Pierides and the type of scandal they tell about the gods fit well with Ovid's own narrator's views, we are left feeling that we might well disagree with the award of victory to the Muses and perhaps wondering whether this is not a satiric glance at the sort of establishment censorship Augustus and the old Rome approved. The song about Ceres is wonderful, but so might the song of the Pierides have been, if we had been allowed to hear it.

We have always to listen carefully to assess the stories Ovid's narrators tell, because they reflect the biases of their narrators. And if Ovid's subnarrators are not entirely to be trusted, what of the central Ovid-narrator, who, as we saw, is one of the main unifying factors in the poem? I think Ovid wants us to be wary of the main narrator as well. He is a storyteller, too, on a grand scale, like Scheherazade, who can go on night after night in order to stay alive, except that he does not get the day off, as she does. The narrator reminds us of his presence throughout the poem in the ways I have mentioned, and he loses no chance to remind us that we are listening to fictions rather than watching events unfold.

The Story Untold

One of the most disturbing characteristics of the narrator of the *Metamorphoses* is his occasional obscurity. Now and then he introduces something that seems irrelevant to the context and so unspecific that the reader has no idea what he is talking about. After the apotheosis of Hercules, for example, comes the statement:

nor had Eurystheus, son of Sthenelus, yet given up his
anger; he was fiercely exercising on the children the
hatred he felt for the father.

[9.273–75]

These lines are Ovid's transition from Hercules' apotheosis
to Alcmene's desire to tell about her labor in giving birth to
Hercules. The story they allude to is Eurystheus's pursuit of
the sons of Hercules, but Ovid does not tell us so, and we
are left wondering what Eurystheus has to do with this part
of Hercules' story. (He is, of course, the man responsible for
Hercules' labors.) A hundred or so lines later, the story of the
sons of Hercules comes up again. After Alcmene has told of
her labor pains and Iole, her granddaughter-in-law, has told
of her sister Dryope's metamorphosis into a lotus, Ovid says:

for on the high threshold stood Iolaus—nearly a boy and
with the suggestion of down on his cheek, changed back
in appearance to early youth.

[9.397–99]

There is no mention of who he is or what his connection with
Hercules is. Iolaus is relevant to Hercules' story: he aided the
sons of Hercules in their struggle with Eurystheus; but Ovid
does not tell us so. Instead, Ovid launches into Hebe's deci-
sion never to rejuvenate anyone again, which turns into a
further nonstory about the sequel to the expedition of the
Seven against Thebes.

More comprehensible (and more interesting) than these
fragments of a sequel to Hercules' story is Ovid's "Theseid."
Theseus slips into the poem for the first time in the final
episode of the story of Medea (7.404ff.). Medea, having per-
formed the acts for which she is famous in mythology—help-
ing Jason win the golden fleece, rejuvenating Jason's father,
Aeson, and, finally, killing Jason's new wife and murdering

her own children—escapes from Corinth to Athens, where she is welcomed and married by Aegeus, Theseus's father. Aegeus had, however, never seen his son, because he left Troezen before Theseus was born. Hence Ovid opens his Theseus nonstory with a clarifying introduction:

> And already Theseus was present (child unknown to his father); he had pacified the Isthmus of two seas through his courage. For his destruction Medea mixed poison which she had brought with her from Scythian shores. . . .
>
> [7.404–7]

Having thus brought Medea and Theseus face to face, Ovid goes off into a 11½-line "digression" about the poison, said to come from the saliva of Cerberus, the guard dog of the Underworld, when Hercules brought him out of the Underworld into the light. So Theseus's story becomes Hercules' story. As the reader wonders confusedly what Hercules and Cerberus are doing here, Ovid returns to the Medea and Theseus story at the moment when Aegeus unwittingly offers the poisoned cup to Theseus. Theseus accepts it, but the father recognizes the young man's ivory sword hilt, the family emblem, in the nick of time, knocks the poison aside, and Medea flees. We have the skeleton of what might have been a story, but it never quite gets told. Lurking behind the few hints Ovid drops (unknown son, family tokens) is the story I outlined at the start. The reader who knows mythology will at least be able to make something of Theseus's prehistory, but anyone, no matter what mythological lore he or she is master of, will be mystified by the little disquisition on Cerberus's saliva hardening into poison. It may seem less surprising, though, when we see what else Ovid does with this tale.

Aegeus, in thanksgiving for the rescue of his son, sacrifices to the gods and celebrates with a feast at which the people sing a hymn to Theseus (wine giving them inspiration, says the poet drily [432–33]). The hymn lists the exploits of Theseus, depicting him as a kind of second Hercules who has purged the world of monsters. Theseus now seems to have been properly introduced, and those who know his story will recognize that Ovid has begun to set the scene for Theseus's most famous exploit, his defeat of the Minotaur.

Let us look quickly at the main points of the story as it was traditionally told so that we can see what Ovid does with it. Minos and Pasiphae were king and queen of Crete. Pasiphae fell in love with a bull (a story Ovid tells in the *Ars*), and the artist Daedalus devised a way for her to consummate her desire, the result of this implausible union being the Minotaur, half-bull, half-man. Androgeos, the son of Minos and Pasiphae, was killed by the Athenians, and Minos went to war with them, finally granting them peace in return for a periodic sacrifice of fourteen young Athenians to the Minotaur. When Theseus came to Crete as one of the hostages, he killed the Minotaur and escaped from the labyrinth in which the Minotaur was housed with the help of Ariadne, the princess who had fallen in love with him and had given him a spool of thread to unwind as he went into the labyrinth so that he would be able to find his way out again, something no one had ever accomplished before. Ariadne and Theseus fled from Crete together, but Theseus deserted her in Naxos on the way back and returned to Athens, having forgotten the promise (made to his father when he left) to change the sails from black to white if he had been successful. Aegeus, seeing black sails, thought his son was dead and threw himself off a cliff into the sea that now bears his name.

Ovid introduces this episode with the remark that Aegeus's joy at recovering his son was short-lived because of the war Minos was preparing in revenge for Androgeos's death. Surprise—Ovid says nothing further at this point

about Theseus, nor does he tell us about Minos. Using Mi-
nos's projected war against Athens as a transition, he carries
us to the island of Aegina, whose people refuse to aid Minos
in his forthcoming war on the grounds of their age-old alliance
with Athens. Thus instead of hearing the story of Theseus
and the Minotaur, we get the beginning of a story about Mi-
nos at war with Athens, further back in time, and then, in-
stead of getting even that story, we are presented with what
sounds as if it might be the introduction to a war between
Aegina and Minos: "That alliance of yours will cost you a lot"
(487)—a very ominous-sounding half-line. The war does not
take place. The rest of the book is filled with a pair of tales:
the Aeginetan king's account of the plague that destroyed the
people of Aegina and the miracle that restored it, and the
Athenian ambassador Cephalus's account of his tragic mar-
riage to Procris.

Theseus has another chance to have his story told in the
next book, in which the Cretan story is picked up again. Mi-
nos is waging war against the city of Megara, whose local
princess, Scylla, falls in love with him and betrays her city to
him. Minos returns home victorious, and Ovid now gives the
barest outline of the famous Minotaur story, narrated in such
a way as to emphasize everybody and everything rather than
Theseus:

> After the labyrinth had shut in the double-figured bull-
> man, and the third lottery, recurring after nine years, had
> tamed the monster twice fed on blood, and as soon as
> the door (never regained by any before) had been found
> by rolling up the thread, thanks to a virgin, straightaway
> the son of Aegeus, seizing Minos's daughter, set sail for
> Naxos and deserted his companion on that shore, cruel
> man . . .
>
> [8.169–76]

(The omitted 6½ lines of this fourteen-line sequence are devoted to Bacchus's rescue of Ariadne and the metamorphosis of her crown into the constellation Corona Borealis.)

If we look for Theseus in the lines that concern him, where do we find him? Implied by the "third lottery," of course, which made him one of the hostages sent to feed the Minotaur, but Theseus is unnamed and his great action has shrunk to a subordinate clause, while most of the credit is assigned to "a virgin." When Theseus is referred to directly, it is as the son of Aegeus, portrayed by a participial phrase as unheroically kidnapping Ariadne, and then by two verbs describing his main actions—*vela dedit*, "he set sail," and *destituit*, "he deserted," with the adjective "cruel" attached. Ovid could hardly have treated him more condescendingly. (The poet does the same thing in his two accounts of the "feats" of Jason in *Heroides* 6.10–14, 32–36. The most specific reference to Jason is to what he did not have to do: "When the seeds were scattered there sprang up a crop of men who did not need your right arm to die" [11–12].)

This is the end of Ovid's nonstory about Theseus. Theseus appears elsewhere in the poem but only as one of many "heroes." He takes part in the comedy of errors produced by the Calydonian boar-hunt, in which his one heroic action is to hurl a "well-aimed spear sure to achieve its goal," which misses and gets caught in a tree; and he brings down one centaur in the battle of Lapiths and Centaurs before vanishing from the poem forever.

How can we explain Ovid's treatment of these stories? It is possible that he did not realize that he never gave a full account of these heroes. Certainly we would not have missed the sons of Hercules, if he had left them out entirely. But Theseus turns up so often in the *Metamorphoses* that the poet's treatment of him seems likely to have been intentional. Did Ovid perhaps especially dislike Theseus and tell his story so obliquely in order to show his distaste? That is not impossible—Theseus was a superhero and might well have seemed more repellent than lesser heroes to Ovid, who, as we have seen, had no use for heroes of any kind. Furthermore, Theseus's story had been overworked—so much so that in the next century Juvenal (ca. A.D. 60–130?) used it as his example of a hackneyed (and boring) subject for public recitation:

> Must I always be in the audience? Can't I, who have been done in again and again by that long-winded "Theseid" of scratchy-voiced Cordus, have a turn?
>
> [Juvenal 1.1–3]

Certainly Ovid was not about to include a conventional "Theseid" in his poem. He was bound to change the emphasis, as he always did when he treated a well-known tale. It should not surprise us that his Theseus is less than heroic, nor that his "Theseid" is only marginally the story of Theseus. We have seen that Ovid experiments with the many ways a story can be told: one way is not to tell it at all. In order to make your reader see that you are not telling it, you have to bring it to his attention and then move off in another direction, and this is what Ovid does with the sons of Hercules and with Theseus. It is not unlike what he does with the story of Aeneas, which, in Ovid's hands, is an account of what Vergil left out.

Arguably, then, Ovid's nonstories are one of his ways of alerting us not to forget that the *Metamorphoses* is fiction. It is a story told by a poet with thousands and thousands of stories at his disposal who, like Homer's bard, shapes them for the occasion and might well, we imagine, shape them entirely differently another time. It is this poet who occupies the center of Ovid's poem. He holds us in his spell, and he breaks the mold of epic objectivity, recreating epic for a new time and a new world with a style of epic that can contain things even as extraneous to epic of the old style as the long didactic speech of Pythagoras with which the poem nears its end.

Pythagoras

I shall close this discussion with Pythagoras (15.60–478)—to my mind Ovid's climax to a succession of unreliable and comic narrators. Pythagoras has a personality and personal interests that need to be examined before we decide how seriously we are going to take him. The fifteen-line sentence in which he is introduced tells us much, I would argue, about Ovid's own attitude toward him. The introducer rushes breathlessly on, spewing out an enormous amount of information that is much too diverse to be comfortably included in one poorly articulated sentence (15.60–74). He does not take Pythagoras seriously enough to distinguish between his origins, his scientific and theological study, and his precepts. A whole course in ancient physics (the causes of things, what nature and what god can do, the source of snow and the origin of lightning, where thunder comes from—Jupiter or wind—what causes earthquakes, the law of stellar motion, and "whatever else is concealed") is crammed into five lines, to which the introducer also appends the concept of metempsychosis and its corollary, vegetarianism. Finally, making obvious what he has been hinting at all along, he concludes with the extraordinary statement:

> and he [Pythagoras] was the first also to open his lips with the following, erudite, to be sure, but no one believed him.
>
> [15.73–74]

After this introduction it should be no surprise to find that the speech itself is a comic grab bag of soapbox philos-

ophy—vehement and impassioned, in the manner of good
didactic poetry, but signifying little. It swarms with bits and
pieces of the philosophies that had attracted ancient thinkers,
including all the more ridiculous aspects of pythagoreanism
while omitting all the most important tenets of the school. It
is, in other words, another burlesque of didactic like the *Ars*,
though tailored in subject and style to epic.

The earlier books of the *Metamorphoses* have shown Ovid
playing off Vergil at every turn. By the fifteenth book he has
rewritten much of the *Aeneid* in his comic vein and gone even
beyond the chronological limits of Vergil's narrative into the
subject of his prophecies. Now he inserts a four-hundred-line
speech by Pythagoras into his account of the second Roman
king (as if Vergil had included the *Georgics* in the framework
of the *Aeneid*). This king—King Numa—is left dangling (in
the dative case, line 10) for half a book and then, after Py-
thagoras's long speech, disposed of summarily (479–87) while
Ovid rushes on to later Roman history and finally to Julius
Caesar and Augustus (760ff.). Here, too, I think we may hear
Ovid's voice saying, "Well, you never thought I could get
away with this one, did you? But I did. I have incorporated
into an "epic" frame a long didactic narration, something
lesser poets would never have tried. And I have made it fit,
because it, like the rest of the poem, is all about change and
so completes the philosophical frame I established in the
opening lines of Book 1. On top of all this, I have capped my
series of unreliable narrators with one nobody could ever have
expected yet who exactly fits his place in my version of Roman
history. My narrator, original to the end, can thus claim, with
a bow to Horace (see *Odes* 3.30.1–7) and an ironic smile in the
direction of Augustus, the new Jupiter:

> And now I have completed a work that neither Jupiter's
> anger, nor fire, nor iron, nor hungry time can obliterate.

Let that day, which has jurisdiction over nothing but this body, end the uncertain space of my life whenever it desires. Still with the better part of me I shall be carried forever above the stars and my name will be indestructible, and where Roman power extends over conquered lands—if the predictions of seers have any truth—I shall live.

[15.871–79]

V OVID, THE POET

OVID TRANSFORMED EVERYTHING HE TOUCHED. USING THE OR-
dinary Latin poetic vocabulary in its simplest forms, he made
it sing in a new way. An Ovidian verse is generally recogniz-
able. As the poet says himself, addressing the first book of
his exile poems and imagining it will soon reach Rome from
Tomis:

> Even if your title is missing, you will be recognized by
> your style; it is clear that you are mine, even if you want
> to hide it.

> [*Tr.* 1.1.61–62]

The word I have translated as style is *color*, which means
something like "quality," "complexion," or "shade," that spe-
cial something that makes someone's appearance distinctive.
We sometimes use "flavor" to get at a similar idea. Ovid's
writing from beginning to end has its own *color*. As with the
texture of a wine, it is easier to perceive than to describe, but
we can at least pick out one major ingredient. Probably the
first word that comes to mind when people think of Ovid is
"wit" (in and out of season, some would say), another is
exuberance. If one word is good, would ten not be better?
And what happens if this word rubs up against that one?
Ovid likes to play with words. I imagine him turning them
over to see what makes them tick, shaking them, and smiling
to himself as he chooses one that does not quite fit its context
to see what effect it has.

Verbal wit can work on many levels; at its lowest, it is merely ingenious, but it *can* open up a world of meaning. Probably the most notorious example of Ovidian wit is a line in the *Ars* describing the Minotaur. Instructing his student on the difficulty of keeping the girl he has won, Ovid claims that Cupid, being winged, is hard to hold, just as Daedalus was, and goes off into the story of Daedalus and Icarus. The narrative begins:

> As soon as Daedalus had imprisoned the mother's criminally conceived half-bull man and half-man bull . . .
>
> [*Ars* 2.23–24]

A fascinating anecdote about the second line of the couplet, *semibovemque virum, semivirumque bovem* (half-bull man and half-man bull), is told by a contemporary of Ovid's, one Albinovanus Pedo (reported in Seneca the Elder's *Controversiae* 2.2.12). Seneca relates the anecdote to prove that Ovid "was not ignorant of his faults; he enjoyed them." According to Pedo, who claimed to be present, Ovid was asked by some friends to let them eliminate three of his verses; he agreed, with the condition that he could choose three over which they would have no jurisdiction. Both parties wrote down their choices—and all three were identical. One of the three was the Minotaur line.

How can we interpret the reasoning of the two parties in this story? Presumably Ovid's friends disliked the Minotaur line because, in their opinion, it showed the poet at his worst, using words merely for the sake of wit. It is just *too* clever. But why should Ovid want the verse preserved? Was he so bad a critic that he thought this one of his best lines? That seems unlikely. In fact, according to the same anecdote, he responded that a face is the more attractive for having a blemish. Probably an element in his choice was, as so often, his desire to shock and challenge. Ovid loved to get a rise out of his audience. But I suspect that if this little comedy really took place, Ovid chose the line because it seemed to him to show something basic about his *color*, and he chose a "bad" line rather than a "good" line because it would make people analyze, scrutinize, and think, as they would otherwise not have done.

In Latin the line, "half-bull man and half-man bull" is perfectly symmetrical, falling into two metrically identical halves: long, short, short; long, short, short; long; pause; long, short, short; long, short, short; long. This is the pentameter in its purest form, each half-line being identical to the other. Latin poets generally tended to avoid this effect by varying the first half-line. Here Ovid actually courts that metrical symmetry; he even chooses to emphasize the split between the half-lines by having a sense pause at the metrical break in the middle. In addition, the words are exactly balanced, and the parallelism is made complete by the presence of *-que* attached to the end of each adjective; *-que* means "and," or, when repeated, "both . . . and," making a five-syllable word out of a four-syllable word in both halves. Thus the Latin is even more startlingly symmetrical than the English, which has "and" only once in the center. The Latin also has more alliteration and assonance than the English can manage because of the repeated *-em, -um, -um, -em,* as well as the *v*-sounds (pronounced like English *w*) of *virum,* and *semivirum, bovem* and *semibovem.*

What are we to make of all this? I would certainly not suggest that this is one of the best lines Ovid ever wrote, but it achieves its limited purpose—it is amusing and it draws attention to itself (and thus to the mind and art of its creator), which is a characteristically Ovidian practice and quite different from, say, that of Vergil. The artificiality in the arrangement of the language brings out the incongruity of the creature: a half-bull/half-man, who is, in this formulation, *ex-*

actly half and half. What is not bull is man and what is not man is bull. Language can do what nature cannot—add half a bull to half a man and get a Minotaur. The rather comical formulation of the Minotaur's mixed nature does not encourage us to linger over him sympathetically (and, in any case, our attention is immediately drawn away from the beast, which is only the object of a subordinate clause). Even so, this rather jocular characterization of the Minotaur reminds us of the partial humanity of the beast, which we otherwise tend to forget when we read the myth in which he figures. Ovid was fascinated by human beings, their affinities with animals, their shifts in identity, their problems of identity, and the nature of metamorphosis. Even the Minotaur, casually dropped into the *Ars* to introduce a digression, offers Ovid a moment of linguistic play with the idea of a mixed identity such as Robert Louis Stevenson put to use in Dr. Jekyll and Mr. Hyde and modern psychology has identified in certain types of schizophrenia.

It is interesting to note that when Ovid recalls this line on the Minotaur much later, in a poem written in exile, he uses only the first part of the line, joining it with a half-line describing another physical impossibility, the hundred-handed giant Gyes: *centimanumque Gyan, semibovemque virum* (*Tr.* 4.7.18). Even Ovid must have thought that once was enough for the bull-man man-bull.

I have perhaps made more of this than it is worth, but it is a line that could only have been written by Ovid, and it is characteristic of Ovidian wit. Now let us look at a more respectable line built on similar principles. This, too, comes from the *Ars Amatoria*, this, too, could only have been written by Ovid, but this one seems to have more to say than the other. At the beginning of the poem, when the Master of Love is setting out his credentials as teacher, he establishes a parallel between his role vis-à-vis Cupid and the relationship

between the centaur Chiron and the boy Achilles. Chiron had
been put in charge of Achilles by his father, Peleus; Ovid had
been put in charge of Cupid by Cupid's mother, Venus. Both
boys were born of goddesses:

saevus / uterque /puer / /natus / uterque / dea

[*Ars* 1.18]

savage / each-one / boy // born / each-one / from-goddess.

Here is a beautifully symmetrical line, each half consisting,
in the Latin, of three words. The first half-line contains a
masculine adjective, a pronoun, and a masculine noun; the
second a masculine participial adjective, the same pronoun,
and the word for goddess in the ablative case, giving the par-
entage of each boy. Once again the pentameter halves are
metrically identical, once again the language is simple, but
here the symmetry suggested by the meter and the grammar
is used for more than merely verbal wit. It points up the
similarity of the two boys, who would seem, on the face of
it, to be as different as night from day. Ovid has made us see
something we would not otherwise have seen by his manip-
ulation of language. Though this is a poetic gift that we as-
sociate above all with Vergil, Ovid here characteristically
shows that it need not always be applied to high-tragic Ver-
gilian ends. He creates a highly amusing line, joining, in a
brilliant verbal pattern, two entities that are worlds apart;
Achilles with his man-slaughtering hands, a character from
epic, and Cupid, the love god from elegy, a warrior of a very
different kind. The union does not work because, of course,
the parallel is not parallel at all, as *we* can see, even though
the instructor does not seem to. The verbal identification ac-
tually emphasizes the contrast between the two realities while
uncovering a deep likeness: both Cupid and Achilles make
war, both elegy and epic are about victory and defeat.

Now let us look at Ovid working with a couplet rather than a single verse. In the *Fasti* he writes about the destruction of 306 members of the family of the Fabii who offered to fight for Rome against the people of Veii. All were killed (except one boy who was too young to go to war):

> una dies / Fabios / ad bellum / miserat / omnes:
> ad bellum / missos // perdidit / una dies;
>
> > [*F.* 2.235–36]

> one day / Fabians / to war / had sent / all /
> to war / having-been-sent [Fabians] // destroyed / one day;

> a single day sent all the Fabians to war:
> a single day destroyed the Fabians sent to war.

The Latin could hardly be simpler or more repetitive. Every element of the first line is repeated in the second, where only one new thought appears: *perdidit,* "destroyed." "One day" opens the couplet, "one day" closes it; within it "one day" of beginning and end contrasts with "all the Fabians" coming at the midpoint. In its own simple way the couplet affects us much as does the historian Livy's moving sentence summing up the destruction of Alba Longa: "and one hour gave to destruction and ruin the work of the four hundred years during which Alba had stood" (*unaque hora quadringentorum annorum opus quibus Alba steterat excidio ac ruinis dedit*) (Livy, *Ab urbe condita* 1.29.6). Both passages neatly contrast the single moment of devastation with the multiplicity and grandeur of what was destroyed.

There is a similar awful simplicity in Phaedra's attempt to convince Hippolytus of the propriety of an affair between stepmother and stepson. Again Ovid is working with the cou-

plet, again he opposes one and more than one, and again he
uses near repetition to get his effect, this time merely chang-
ing perfect tenses to future tenses:

> ut tenuit / domus una / duos, / domus una / tenebit;
> oscula aperta / dabas, // oscula aperta / dabis;
>
> [*Her.* 4.143–44]

> just as has held / one house / two, / one house / will
> hold [two];
> kisses openly / you gave, // kisses openly / you will
> give.

> just as one house has held two, one house will hold
> two;
> you gave kisses openly, you will give kisses openly.

In Phaedra's formulation everything will be exactly as it has
been—the two of them have lived together in some intimacy,
and they will continue to do so. All the externals will be the
same, but their significance will be totally different, and the
sameness of language points up Phaedra's moral blindness.
We see what Phaedra attempts to conceal, the horrendous
difference between appearance and realities.

Ovid builds whole episodes on the conflict between lan-
guage and reality. In *Metamorphoses* 10.298ff., Orpheus tells
the tale of Myrrha's passion for her father, Cinyras. Through-
out this tale Ovid has Orpheus play with the paradoxical na-
ture of words. When Myrrha confesses her desire for her
father and recognizes that it is wrong, she expresses the close-
ness of the family tie that forbids the sort of intimacy she
desires with the words, "now, because he is already mine, he
is not mine" (339). Mine cannot be mine. This is witty, play-
ful, but also moving, and it makes us think about the rela-
tionship between language and reality.

When Myrrha struggles to give up all thoughts of her

father, everything conspires against her, even the Latin language—allowing her to speak one truth only to have it received as a very different truth. Asked by her father what sort of husband she wants, she blushes and says, "like you" (364): a confession of guilt mistaken as filial piety, for which she is warmly praised. Piety and crime should be opposites, but the words have got confused, and that confusion is, as Orpheus makes us see, basic to the human condition. When the incestuous union is about to take place (line 465), Orpheus brings Myrrha and Cinyras together in a line that perfectly represents the situation:

accipit / obsceno // genitor / sua viscera / lecto,

receives / in obscene // father / his own flesh / bed.

The father receives his own flesh in the incestuous bed.

In the Latin, the verb comes first, the adjective, "incestuous" or "obscene" (*obsceno*), comes next, closely followed by the word for father—and the word chosen is *genitor*, emphasizing the father as "begetter." *Sua viscera* is used metaphorically for "daughter" but it actually means a person's own vitals and brings out the abnormality of a father united with the flesh of his flesh. Finally, the word for bed (*lecto*) picks up the adjective, "incestuous," adjective and noun surrounding father and daughter just as the incestuous bed embraces the unholy pair. Piece by piece the stones are placed until the mosaic is complete.

When Cinyras belatedly decides to find out who the partner of his bed has been these last nights, Orpheus reveals all:

                    inlato lumine / vidit
          et scelus / et natam
                    light having been brought in / he saw
          both crime / and daughter.

Ovid brings together the two apparently unlike, nonparallel objects in such a way that the two become one. The grammatical joining of the two nouns serves as the "recognition scene" (anagnorisis) familiar to us from Greek tragedy, the moment when the protagonist finally understands the truth, as Cinyras sees and understands in a flash. Once again Ovid is asking us to think about the nature of experience and of language. We have come a long way from the merely verbal play of the Minotaur verse, but we are still far from what Vergil might have written. The neat packaging of the parallel "both crime and daughter" cuts into the pathos of the situation and nudges it toward comedy. It disposes of incest in a rather flippant manner characteristic of Ovid's speaker, who is seldom totally serious, particularly when he is moving toward a new story, as he is doing here.

In every context, whether Ovid is being playful or serious, his language is designed to draw attention to itself in a way that Vergil's never does. Hyperbole, paradox, oxymoron, zeugma, antithesis, parenthesis, irrelevant or unnecessary comments, changes of direction, incongruities between subject and style—these are hallmarks of Ovid's style; all focus our attention on *how* what is said is said, and thus on the language itself. It was Plato, speaking for Socrates in the *Apology*, who said that the unexamined life is not worth living and who was concerned that people should learn to distinguish between reality and appearance. But Plato wanted to banish poets and poetry from his Republic, and certainly Ovid would have been one of the first to go. Yet Ovid is as concerned as Plato with reality and appearance, and the poet (in his own way) devotes as much time to the subject as the philosopher.

If Ovid has a message, it is perhaps something like this: do not believe anything without looking at it carefully; particularly question those who make great claims for themselves, for there is no such thing as The Truth, there are only

individual truths, and these, too, are mutable. Even if some-
one is trying to tell you his truth (and he may well not be),
words are slippery creatures. (It is noteworthy that a common
Latin expression for deceiving is "to give words," *verba dare*.)
Words are deceptive whether or not the speaker intends to
deceive, as Ovid knew (and relished the knowledge), and as
we are frequently reminded in our own lives when we con-
clude a conversation realizing that we have been talking at
cross-purposes all the time. Of course, often a speaker *does*
intend his words to deceive or at least to obscure harsh real-
ities. The speaker of the *Ars* is a master of deception; in fact,
the art of love as he expounds it is essentially an art of du-
plicity and self-deception. As for us, our daily news consists
of obfuscation through language, from the well-known dis-
tortions of language in Nazi propaganda in the 1930s and
1940s, to "I misspoke myself" (= I lied) of the 1970s, to "our
policy toward Iran was flawed, mistakes were made" (= we
sent large shipments of arms to Iran in spite of our avowed
policy against terrorism, and we secretly aided the Contras
with the profits). But if words can deceive and conceal, they
can also reveal, sometimes against the intention of the
speaker, as when Nestor unmasks heroic society in *Metamor-
phoses* 12 or the professor of love his silly pretensions in the
Ars. Ovid's poems explore the way language corresponds or
fails to correspond to the reality it attempts to present, as the
couplets we looked at earlier and as his experiments with
narrators show.

   But Ovid would not approve our taking him too seriously
any more than he approved pretensions and pomposity in
others. The only thing Ovid consistently takes seriously him-
self is poetry. Perhaps Ovid's greatest and most irreplaceable
gift to Western literature has been his spirit, his élan, his *color*
(in a broader sense than that in which we were using it ear-

lier). Spirits are notoriously difficult to catch, and none is more elusive than Ovid's. Still let us try. If we were to read Ovid's couplet predicting his death and burial in Tomis:

> inter Sarmaticas Romana vagabitur umbras,
> perque feros Manes hospita semper erit,
>
> [*Tr.* 3.3.63–64]
>
> among Sarmatian souls will wander a Roman soul, forever a foreigner among fierce spirits,

we would know we were reading Ovid, even if the subject did not tell us. The couplet has typically Ovidian ingredients: wit, incongruity, and paradox, but so do many verses in, say, Martial; what seems to me to make this couplet uniquely Ovidian is its vision—its blend of laughter and tears. The notion of a specifically Roman soul preserving its Romanness and Sarmatian souls their fierceness even after death is funny. We have to smile at the thought of that poor Roman soul trapped forever among foreigners, an incongruity that surely no one but Ovid would have dreamed up; yet it brings a shudder as well, because it captures the longing of a Roman exile to return to his kind, the horror of an eternity of wandering in fear and feeling out of place. This may not be high tragedy, but it is poignant and moving, and it has stuck in my mind ever since I first read it. (I hope it is not true; I hope Ovid is conversing happily somewhere with poets and maybe even philosophers, as Socrates imagined himself doing in the *Apology.*)

The human comedy, as Ovid sees it, holds much laughter and many tears, often at the same time. Seldom do we read more than a few verses before Ovidian laughter bubbles up; we come to expect it every time his subject or his style begins to soar. And so it is that Deucalion and Pyrrha (*Meta.* 1) make us smile (as their cousins, Mr. and Mrs. Noah, do not). For all their virtue they are a bit slow of wit, especially Pyrrha, who is the daughter of Epimetheus, the "after-thinker"; being rather literal-minded she is distressed at the oracle's command to throw her mother's bones around, until her more intelligent husband, son of Prometheus, the "fore-thinker," convinces her that the bones are stones. Phaëthon's story (*Meta.* 2), while reminding us of the dangers of overreaching (and of making promises without considering the consequences), has a great deal of comedy in it (who but Ovid would have given the detail that Phaëthon did not even know the names of the horses of the Sun as one of the reasons for his inability to manage them). Baucis and Philemon are exemplary mortals, good, honest, and devoted to each other, but we have to smile at them all the same, especially when old Philemon hobbles after the goose he wants to sacrifice for Jupiter (*Meta.* 8). Even Cadmus and Harmonia, who play a minute part in Ovid's comedy, have their moment of comic sadness, as Cadmus turns into a snake before his wife's eyes:

> "Come, unhappy wife, come," he said, "and while there is still something left of me, touch me; take my hand while I still have a hand, and snake hasn't yet taken me over entirely."
>
> [*Meta.* 4.583–85]

Before he can finish speaking, his tongue forks into a snake's, and his wife calls:

> "Cadmus, stay, unhappy one, take off that monster, Cadmus, what is this? where's your foot, where are your shoulders and hands. . . ." She had spoken; he licked his wife's face, moving into her beloved embrace as if he recognized it.
>
> [591–96]

There is something very moving about this depiction of human love triumphing over metamorphosis. Ovid can touch the heart while making us smile at man's follies and frailties.

Perhaps the key to Ovid's spirit, if there is one, is his airy mocking freedom. Ovid refuses to be fettered by anything, by the restrictions of hexameter and elegiac verse, which he makes move with a speed and grace with which it had never moved before, by the distinctions of genre, which he broke down to allow Latin verse to do things it had never done before, or by the sobriety of the Augustan regime, whose sacred cows were no match for his irreverence. He is a free spirit who "does his own thing," whatever the consequences to poetry or to himself.

The consequences for Latin poetry were, in general, that when Ovid was finished with a genre, nothing remained to do with it, at least until a later day in a different language. His *Amores* have no Latin successors, but they inspired John Donne. His *Heroides* are unique in Latin, but they opened up a popular genre in English: Michael Drayton's *Englands Heroicall Epistles* and Alexander Pope's *Eloisa to Abelard*, to take a more famous example. The *Ars*, too, was enormously influential among poets of later ages, but there is no trace of any descendants of it in Classical Latin literature. The *Fasti* remains unique; as far as I know no one has tried to pick up where Ovid left off. Although Roman poets continued to write epic (Lucan's *Civil War*, Valerius Flaccus's *Argonautica*, Silius Italicus's *Thebaid*, for example), no one attempted to challenge the *Metamorphoses* as Ovid had challenged the *Aeneid* or Vergil the Homeric poems; nor, for all its enormous influence on Western literature, does the *Metamorphoses* have any poetic heirs, although Milton's *Paradise Lost* is, perhaps, comparable in largeness of vision. It should not surprise anyone that the poems from exile had no Roman successors, and yet an eleventh- or twelfth-century French poet responded with a poetic letter from Florus to Ovid in exile (Baudri de Bourgeuil, *Oeuvres poétiques*), and in 1922 the Russian poet Osip Mandelstam published a collection of poems called *Tristia*, its title taken from a poem modeled in part on Ovid's *Tristia* 1.3.

The consequences of Ovid's free spirit for himself were, of course, exile from Rome. Would he have written differently if he had known what was to come? He writes as if he would have in some of the poems from exile, but there he also writes as if the *Metamorphoses* were a poem in praise of Augustus, which it can only be said to be if we assume that good poetry is a celebration of the age that produced it.

VI   I SHALL LIVE

LIKE ALL GREAT POETS OVID LIVES ON IN HIS POETRY; UNLIKE many poets he also lives in the painting and sculpture, the music and literature his magic inspired from his day to our own. A walk though most art galleries or a look at any volume of Old Masters brings us face to face with recreations of Ovid's words—we see Philemon and Baucis (*Metamorphoses* 8) in a Rembrandt, Venus and her beloved Adonis (*Meta.* 10) in a Titian, the lovely sea nymph Galatea (*Meta.* 13) in a Raphael, and innumerable Ovidian characters and scenes in Rubens's mythological paintings. In sculpture Bernini's famous statue of Daphne turning into a laurel tree comes right out of *Metamorphoses* 1 and Michelangelo's battle of Lapiths and Centaurs out of *Metamorphoses* 12. Tapestries, frescoes, fountains, even cathedral doors, such as those designed by the fifteenth-century sculptor Filarete for Saint Peter's (and we really might have expected that cathedral doors at least would have been reserved for Christian stories)—all these have offered space over the centuries for Ovid's tales, and many remain to be enjoyed today.

More surprising than Ovid's ubiquity in art, perhaps, is his presence in music. Although it is difficult to imagine what the effect would have been, Ovid's poems were performed on stage, as I mentioned in chapter 1. About fifteen hundred years later Bartolomeo Tromboncino set Ovid's letter from Dido to Aeneas (*Heroides* 7) to music. And Bach took the story of the contest between Apollo and Pan, *Der Streit zwischen*

Phoebus und Pan, from *Metamorphoses* 11. As any opera lover knows, early European opera would be inconceivable without Ovid as a rich source of plots. Handel's *Acis and Galatea* (with its delightful libretto by Gay) is, perhaps, the most famous of the operas based on Ovid, but there are many others, including a fifteenth-century Cephalus, a sixteenth-century Daphne, and seventeenth-, eighteenth-, and ninteenth-century versions of the story of Orpheus and Eurydice. Even in the twentieth century, where we see relatively little influence from the Classics, Richard Strauss's *Daphne* and Benjamin Britten's "Six Metamorphoses after Ovid" (for solo oboe) owe their inspiration to Ovid.

It is when we turn to literature, of course, that we find Ovid everywhere. His influence on English poetry is so profound that we can hardly pick up an anthology of any date without finding his tracks. Back in the fourteenth century Chaucer knew his Ovid: his first poem was a version of Ovid's Ceyx and Alcyone (*Meta.* 11); the great antifeminist book that the Wife of Bath's fifth husband used to read, to her annoyance, and that she finally made him burn, contained, among other works, Ovid's *Art of Love;* and Ovid's statue is prominent (along with Vergil's, Lucan's, and Claudian's) in the *House of Fame.*

The sixteenth century was visibly an Age of Ovid. Edmund Spenser's allegorical figure of Morpheus, or Sleep, "whom drowned deepe / In drowsie fit he findes" (*Faerie Queen* 1.40.8–9) is right out of *Metamorphoses* 11, while his lovers, Paridell and Hellenore (3.10ff.), come from Ovid's *Heroides* 16 and 17, the correspondence between Paris and Helen. The next pair of letters in the *Heroides* gave Christopher Marlowe the starting point for his *Hero and Leander,* which is stunningly Ovidian in tone. Ovid is thoroughly at home in Shakespeare. As L. P. Wilkinson points out, hardly a play by Shakespeare does not show Ovidian influence. In the view of

Francis Meres, *Paladis Tamia* (1598), "the sweete wittie soul of Ovid lives in mellifluous and honey-tongued Shakespeare." Ovid is held up as the model of the true poet in *Love's Labours Lost:*

> Here are only numbers ratified; but for the
> elegancy, facility, and golden cadence of poesy,
> *caret.* Ovidius Naso was the man. And why, indeed,
> Naso, but for the jerks of invention?
>
> [4.2]

and a version of his Pyramus and Thisbe is the play performed by the "mechanicals" in *A Midsummer Night's Dream.* (In fact, the whole of that play, with its magical world of flight, pursuit, and transformation, is Ovidian in atmosphere. So is the fairy tale world of *The Tempest,* and indeed Prospero's invocation of the spirits of magic in act 5 comes from Arthur Golding's translation of *Metamorphoses* 7.192–219, where Medea calls for help with her magic spells.)

John Donne's verse letter "Sappho to Philaenis" has Ovid's letter from Sappho to her lover in its background, and Donne's Sappho even refers to her former love for Phaon, the young man she addresses in *Heroides* 15, in a verse letter extolling the love of woman for woman. Donne's song "The Sun Rising" has as its starting point Ovid's elegy, *Amores* 1.13, addressed by the lover to the Dawn, begging her to delay her arrival so he can stay in bed with his love, and his epigrams are addressed to Ovidian characters: Niobe, Pyramus and Thisbe, and Hero and Leander. Even Milton borrows again and again from the *Metamorphoses* in his *Paradise Lost,* a poem most of us would associate with Vergilian sobriety rather than Ovidian frivolity, and the poem remained one of Milton's favorites throughout his life, frequently read to him in his old age.

John Dryden, too, though he found much to criticize in

Ovid, knew his poetry intimately, and one of the last efforts
of his life was to translate parts of the *Metamorphoses* to go
with his translations of Chaucer and Boccaccio in his *Fables*,
published in 1700. Alexander Pope was a great admirer of
Ovid's and drew on his poems from the early *Pastorals* (1709)
to the *Essay on Man* (1733–34). We can feel Ovid's presence
along with Vergil's in *Windsor Forest*; it seems likely that *The
Rape of the Lock*, Pope's delightful miniature mock-epic, was
based, at least in part, on Ovid's epic parody of Perseus and
Andromeda in *Metamorphoses* 4 and 5, and his Eloisa, in *Eloisa
to Abelard*, is in many ways an Ovidian heroine.

Keats and Shelley were both influenced by Ovid, as was
Byron, who, of all poets who have written in English, is per-
haps the closest in outlook and style. Much of the wit in his
Don Juan has an Ovidian ring. The poet who summed up
mankind's pursuits by claiming that nothing (not sherbet, not
spring water, not burgundy) can:

> After long travel, ennui, love or slaughter
> Vie with that draught of hock and soda water,
>
> [2.180]

has an Ovidian soul, and, indeed, when Byron thought of
love poetry, he thought of Ovid:

> When amatory poets sing their loves
>   In liquid lines mellifluously bland,
> And pair their rhymes as Venus yokes her doves,
>   They little think what mischief is at hand;
> The greater their success the worse it proves,
>   As Ovid's verse may give to understand.
>
> [5.1]

More recently Tennyson, T. S. Eliot, and Ezra Pound have
shown their appreciation of Ovid. "Catullus, Propertius, Hor-
ace and Ovid are the people who matter," wrote Pound in a

letter in 1916. It would be impossible to overestimate Ovid's impact on writers of English. Nor was his influence, of course, limited to English speakers. Dante, Petrarch, Boccaccio, Ariosto, and Tasso in Italian, Goethe and Rilke in German, Ronsard, Corneille, Racine, and Valéry in French, Camões in Portuguese, Cervantes, Lope de Vega, and Calderon in Spanish—all owe him something. Seldom has one poet offered so much to so many in such a variety of languages, periods, and types of poetry.

It is hardly surprising that poets and other artists have, through the ages, found so much to inspire them in Ovid's poems; we are likely to be much more surprised at the impact of his poetry on theologians, philosophers, and moralists until at least the sixteenth century. His poetry survived the early Christian period despite its subject matter; it may not have been ecclesiastically esteemed, at least not publicly, but it was copied frequently enough in the monasteries to ensure the survival of most of it. Predictably, strange things happened to it along the way. Ovid would have been surprised (and, doubtless, amused) by some of the readings his devoted followers devised in order to moralize his texts and make them respectable. A bishop around the time of Charlemagne, for example, quotes a line describing the novice in seduction: "You who come now for the first time to battle, a novice soldier" (*Ars* 1.36) and applies it (only changing Ovid's second person singular to a third person) to the novice in monastic life—a transformation as staggering as any in the *Metamorphoses*.

By this time Ovid also serves as an authority on behavior and morals, often in conjunction with the Scriptures. When in the twelfth century the great theologian and teacher Peter Abelard quotes a verse from Ovid's *Amores* to warn against excessive strictness in monastic rule, we may wonder whether he remembers where it came from. He *seems* to know, because he begins his quotation, "as the poet says," and goes on to quote *Amores* 3.4.17: "We always strive for what is forbidden and desire what is denied." Can he have remembered the context? In *Amores* 3.4, Ovid urges a husband not to keep such a strict watch over his wife, since this only makes her more attractive to outsiders. After all, the speaker goes on to say, it is "boorish" in a husband to be upset by adultery: one must move with the times, and, besides, adultery is good business; from the lover's presents the whole household will profit. Can Abelard have remembered all this when he used Ovid's line? It seems less than likely.

What are we to think when we read that James I of Aragon, in the thirteenth century, opened an assembly of barons and bishops with a text from Scripture (so he tells us in his chronicle), and the "Scripture" was really a line from Ovid's *Ars Amatoria*? The line he said he was citing from the Bible was the Roman poet's advice to the young seducer-in-training about how to hang on to the woman of his choice once he has found her: "Nor is it less a talent to protect what you have than to find it" (2.13). Obviously, Ovid's line had become proverbial, a cultural metamorphosis that would have delighted him. His own *Metamorphoses,* with its wonderful collection of myths from Greece and Rome, offered a yet more fertile field for allegorization and moralization than his explicitly erotic works. Stories that seemed risqué were not, in those days, omitted, or collected at the end of the volume (as was sometimes done by Victorian and early twentieth-century editors; there is, for example, an edition of the first four books of the *Metamorphoses* published in 1875 "expurgated and intended for female schools," edited by N. C. Brooks, president of the Baltimore Female College). Instead, potentially offensive material was explained in such a way that it ceased to be offensive.

For example, in a twelfth-century manuscript from Te-
gernsee is found an anonymous poem in Latin in which the
author attempts to convince an audience of nuns that the
Metamorphoses, despite its subject matter, is acceptable reading
for them. The love stories of the gods, if properly interpreted,
are in very good taste! And *Ovide moralisé*, an early four-
teenth-century poem in Old French based on the *Metamor-
phoses*, retells, with interesting additions, most of Ovid's
poem, while explaining it. The author offers several interpre-
tations of "what this fable means" when he comes to Ovid's
story of Io (*Meta.* 1.583ff.). As Ovid tells it, it is a pretty sordid
story of divine immorality and vindictiveness, the second in
a series of gods raping or attempting to rape mortal girls.
Jupiter, king of the gods, catches sight of the nymph Io,
daughter of a river-god, lusts after her and rapes her, gath-
ering clouds around them to conceal the act from Juno. But
the queen of the gods, used to her philandering husband's
ways, comes down to earth to investigate the cloud, where-
upon Jupiter turns Io into a cow in order to conceal what he's
been up to. Juno, not deceived for a minute, asks for the cow
as a present and turns it over to Argus of the one hundred
eyes to guard. Finally Jupiter, in pity for Io, sends for his son
Mercury to kill Argus (which Mercury does by putting Argus
to sleep with a boring story and cutting off his head). Io flees
to Egypt pursued by gadflies sent by the angry Juno. There
she bears Jupiter's son Epaphus and is henceforward wor-
shipped as the Egyptian goddess Isis.

Christians could not accept such a story literally—gods
could not behave so foully—and so found ways to interpret
the story to mean something different from what it says. The
most interesting of the interpretations offered by the author
of *Ovide moralisé* takes Jupiter to be a king and Io to be a
priestess who loses her virginity (the cow's horns being a sign
of her degraded state). Argus stands for the world, to which

Io is abandoned after her fall, his one hundred eyes corre-
sponding to the delights the world offers to sinners. Io's wan-
derings reflect her bestial pursuit of pleasure. Mercury
represents the eloquence of sermons that save Io, while her
transformation into Isis shows that she was saved from iniq-
uity through repentance. Pierre Bersuirre, in his Latin *Ovidius
moralizatus*, a fourteenth-century commentary on Ovid, offers
still different interpretations of Io's story. Io is the Christian
community, Juno the Church, and Jupiter the Devil. Juno-
church entrusts Io-Christian community to Argus-priests.
Mercury represents the flatterers who lure us away from the
church as Argus falls down on the job. Another possibility is
that Argus represents—not priests but the Devil! And Mer-
cury is Christ.

We are likely to smile at such attempts to explain Ovid's
stories, but we all interpret poems in the light of our own
prejudices and those of the times we live in, and, since this
sort of allegorization allowed Ovid to be read and loved in
ages that might otherwise have spurned him, it was much
less detrimental than the myth that nineteenth- and twen-
tieth-century scholars created about him. According to this
reading Ovid is definitely not a moralist; in fact, he is merely
a clever stylist, a first-rate manipulator of words. This view
arose in part, I think, because his surface is so brilliant that
scholars failed to see that anything lay beneath it and because
they tended to compare Ovid with Vergil and to find him
inferior in failing to do what Vergil did so brilliantly. As T. F.
Higham neatly put it in 1934: "Ovid died for at least the third
time in the nineteenth century and was buried under moun-
tains of disparaging comment to make a throne for Vergil"
(*Classical Review* [1934]: 120). Today we can see that Ovid had
different things to say and a different way (an essentially
comic mode, in contrast to Vergil's essentially tragic mode) of
saying them. We can conclude that Ovid had as much to say

in his own way as does Vergil in his and that our sense of
Rome in the days of the emperor Augustus (or indeed of life
at any date) will be lopsided if we listen only to Vergil and
not to Ovid.

METRICAL APPENDIX

LATIN VERSE IS VERY DIFFERENT FROM ENGLISH VERSE. As GILBERT Murray contrasts the two in "Poesis and Mimesis" (*Essays and Addresses* [1921]): "Our metres are most inconspicuous: as a rule they are only types to which we approximate with as much or as little exactitude as we find convenient. Our poetry is apt to slip out like a stream of wet mud or concrete; theirs was built and fitted, chip by chip, block by block, of hard marble." English verse is made up of a certain number of stressed syllables in a line, the number of stresses determining the type of line. Iambic pentameter, for example, is a line with five stressed syllables in which an unstressed or lightly stressed syllable alternates with a stressed syllable:

> The Knave of Diamonds tries his wily Arts,
> And wins (oh shameful Chance) the Queen of Hearts.
> > [Alexander Pope, *The Rape of the Lock* 3.87–88]

Latin verse, by contrast, consists of combinations of long and short syllables rather than of stressed and unstressed syllables. Each syllable in Latin is either long or short, depending on the length of the vowel in it. All Latin vowels can be either long or short, and the meaning of a word can change with a change in vowel length. Thus *mălum* means "bad" while *mālum* means "apple," so a *mălum mālum* is a bad apple. A syllable containing a short vowel is generally lengthened if the vowel is followed by two consonants, even if the consonants belong to different words. For example, in Ovid's first line of the *Metamorphoses: Īn nŏvă | fērt ănĭ|mūs mū|tātās | dīcĕrĕ | fōrmās*, the short -i- of *in* is lengthened by the -n- of *in* and the -n- of *nova*; the short -e- of *fert* is lengthened by -rt-, and the short -u- of *animus* by the -s- of *animus* and the -m- of *mutatas*. The other long syllables contain vowels that are long by nature: in *mutatas* the first -a- is always long; the second -a- is long because the feminine accusative plural ending *-as-* has a long -a-. (The second -a- of the feminine singular nominative, *mutata,* in contrast, is short.)

Ovid writes in two meters that are closely related but can create contrasting effects: the dactylic hexameter and the elegiac couplet. A dactylic hexameter is a line of verse consisting of six feet, or measures, each of which is either a dactyl (a long syllable followed by two short syllables, ¯˘˘) or a spondee (two long syllables, ¯¯). If we think of a long syllable as a half note in music, a short syllable will be a quarter note; in other words, each foot consists of either two half notes (spondee) or one half note followed by two quarter notes (dactyl). Dactylic hexameter lines are usually grouped with other dactylic hexameter lines to make up phrases, paragraphs, and poems. Sometimes poems in dactylic hexameter are quite short (Vergil's *Eclogues* or Horace's *Satires,* for example); dactylic hexameter is also the meter of epic in Greek and Latin and can run to thousands of lines. Different poets structure their hexameter lines differently. More spondees make a line weightier and slower moving (Vergil's preference), more dactyls give it more forward momentum and create a more tripping effect (Ovid's preference). Basically, however, every dactylic hexameter has the same ingredients as every other. The first four feet can be either dactyls or spondees, the fifth, except in special and noteworthy cases, is always a dactyl, and the sixth is always two syllables, therefore effectively a spondee, although the last syllable can be short, making the final foot ¯˘, in which case a pause fills out the time. Thus many combinations of dactyls and spondees are available to the poet, although it is rare to find more than two or three dactyls or spondees in a row.

The first line of an elegiac couplet is an ordinary dactylic hexameter, the second a truncated one. The couplet looks like this:

¯˘˘ / ¯˘˘ / ¯˘˘ / ¯˘˘ / ¯˘˘ / ¯¯
¯˘˘ / ¯˘˘ / ¯ // ¯˘˘ / ¯˘˘ / ¯

In other words, the second, pentameter (= five feet) line, is a hexameter with a half-foot missing at the midpoint and a half-foot missing at the end. This line falls into two equal halves and has a break in the middle. The second half of the pentameter is always ¯˘˘ / ¯˘˘ / ¯, the first half can vary. It can be ¯¯ / ¯˘˘ / ¯ or ¯¯ / ¯¯ / ¯ or ¯˘˘ / ¯¯ / ¯ or it can be identical to the second half-line, ¯˘˘ / ¯˘˘ / ¯. So, when Ovid claims in *Amores* 1.1 that Cupid has stolen a foot, he speaks the truth: the second line of every couplet is one foot shorter than the first. For the same reason his personified Elegy in *Amores* 3.1 has one foot shorter than the other, and his Muse, Thalia, is carried on uneven wheels (*Ars* 1.264).

Elegiac couplets can be used for extended narrative, as in the *Fasti*, but they seem best suited for shorter verse forms. Catullus, who wrote elegiacs a generation or so before Ovid, worked against the inherent autonomy of the couplet by allowing the sense to run on from couplet to couplet and by avoiding a sense pause at the break in the center of the second verse. Ovid, on the other hand, emphasized the couplet structure. His couplets tend to stand alone with major pauses separating them from each other. He also often turns his couplets in on themselves by using the second verse to point up, or comment on, the first, not to add a new idea.

Although elegiac couplets were generally regarded as less grand than dactylic hexameters, they can be very moving, as Ovid shows when he laments the death of his fellow elegist, Tibullus:

> Memnona si mater, mater ploravit Achillem,
>   et tangunt magnas tristia fata deas,
> flebilis indignos, Elegeia, solve capillos!
>   a, nimis ex vero nunc tibi nomen erit!—
>
>   [*Am.* 3.9.1–4]

If the Dawn wept for her son Memnon, and Thetis for Achilles, and great goddesses are moved by the sadness of death, weep, Elegy, and loosen your undeserving locks—alas, all too truly named are you now.

BIBLIOGRAPHY

FOUR GOOD GENERAL BOOKS IN ENGLISH ON OVID'S POEMS ARE HER-
mann Fränkel, *Ovid, A Poet between Two Worlds* (Berkeley, 1945); E. K.
Rand, *Ovid and His Influence* (1925; reprint, New York, 1963); L. P.
Wilkinson, *Ovid Recalled* (Cambridge, 1955), of which his *Ovid Sur-
veyed* (Cambridge, 1962) is an abbreviated version; and John Barsby's
Ovid (Oxford, 1978), which contains brief and interesting essays on
all of Ovid's poems. E. J. Kenney's article, "Ovid," in the *Cambridge
History of Classical Literature*, vol. 2, part 3: *The Age of Augustus* (Cam-
bridge, 1982), is a good survey. Readers interested in the *Metamor-
phoses* may consult G. Karl Galinsky's *Ovid's Metamorphoses* (Berkeley,
1975), which asks a number of interesting questions about the poem.
Also of interest is Brooks Otis's *Ovid as an Epic Poet*, 2d ed. (Cam-
bridge, 1970), which contains good discussions of many of the longer
love stories. I particularly recommend his treatment of Ceyx and
Alcyone (Book 11) and of Cephalus and Procris (Book 7). Good
books on the *Heroides* are Howard Jacobson's *Ovid's Heroides* (Prince-
ton, 1974) and Florence Verducci's *Ovid's Toyshop of the Heart* (Prince-
ton, 1985). Surprisingly, no book treats Ovid's love poetry in detail,
although the last two chapters of Georg Luck's *The Latin Love Elegy*
(London, 1969) deal with Ovid and R. O. A. M. Lyne's *The Latin
Love Poets* (Oxford, 1980) contains some good discussions of the
Amores. On the *Ars Amatoria* there is Molly Myerowitz's *Ovid's Games
of Love* (Detroit, 1985). Not surprisingly, there is no book on the *Fasti*.
Betty Rose Nagle's *The Poetics of Exile* (Brussels, 1980) is very useful
for the exile poems.

Ovid's works are all available in the Loeb Classical Library series
published by Harvard University Press. I recommend these to any-
one who knows even a little Latin, because the translation faces the
Latin text. Though the translations are not elegant, they are readable.

A choice of translations into modern English is available for the
Metamorphoses. Rolfe Humphries's verse translation, *Ovid, Metamor-*

phoses (Bloomington, Ind., 1955), is the one I generally recommend because it is, on the whole, very readable, although it omits things and has an unfortunate tendency at times to use dated slang. Those who prefer prose translations will probably enjoy *The Metamorphoses of Ovid* by Mary Innes in the Penguin series (1955). Both of these are available in paperback. A new verse translation, which I have so far only had time to browse in, is A. D. Melville's *Ovid, Metamorphoses* (Oxford, 1986). The *Ars Amatoria* and *Amores* have been translated into verse by Humphries in a volume called *The Art of Love* (Bloomington, Ind., 1957), by Peter Green (*The Erotic Poems* [Penguin 1983]), and by Horace Gregory in a volume called *Love Poems of Ovid* (Mentor 1962). Also in print is a good translation (together with the Latin text and notes) of the *Amores* by Guy Lee (London, 1968). No easily available translations of Ovid's other works exist except those in the Loeb series. Readers who enjoy heroic couplets might like to look at the translations by Alexander Pope (selections from *Metamorphoses* 9 and 14 as well as a very free translation of *Heroides* 15, "Sapho to Phaon"), Christopher Marlowe (*Ovid's Elegies*), John Dryden (*Metamorphoses* 1 and selections from other books), or A. E. Watts, whose *The Metamorphoses of Ovid* came out in 1980; the original hardback edition was published in 1954.

In order to avoid unwieldy footnotes in the body of the book I did not give full references for some of the works I mentioned. Since some readers might like further information about them I shall give complete references here. The text of Petrarch's *De vita solitaria*, mentioned on p. 83, is in *Francesco Petrarcha Prose*, ed. G. Martellotti et al., *La letteratura italiana storia e testi*, vol. 7 (Milan and Naples, 1955). The quotation is found on p. 532. Pherecydes' account of Cephalus and Procris, discussed on pp. 132–33, can be found in *Fragmenta historicorum graecorum*, ed. Carl Müller (Paris, 1928): Pherecydis fragmenta, 77. Apollodorus's version of the tale can be found in the same volume; it also appears in the Loeb: *Apollodorus, The Library*, 3.15.1. Hyginus's Cephalus and Procris is in *Hygini fabulae*, ed. H. J. Rose (Leiden, 1963). A discussion of Pope's *The Rape of the Lock* and Ovid's "Perseid" (referred to on p. 162) can be found in G. C. F. Plowden, *Pope on Classic Ground* (Athens, Ohio, 1983). Bishop Theodulf's use of *Ars* 1.36 for the novice monk (referred to on p. 163) appears in "Ad monachos sancti benedicti," *Carmina*, book 2, *Patrologiae cursus completus, Series Latina*, vol. 105, ed. J. P. Migne (Paris, 1864), p. 312.

Abelard's quotation of *Amores* 3.4.17 (referred to on pp. 163–64) can be found in *The Letters of Abelard and Heloise* (Penguin, 1974), Letters of Direction #7, 2.39. Letter #5, referred to on p. 83, is also included in that volume. James I's attribution to the Bible of a line from Ovid's *Ars* (discussed on p. 164), is on p. 507 of *The Chronicle of James I, King of Aragon*, trans. John Forster, vol. 2, 388 (London, 1883). The anonymous Latin poem mentioned on p. 165 can be found in Wattenbach, "Zwei Handschriften der k. Hof- und Staatsbibliothek," *Sitzungberichte der philosophisch-philologischen und historischen Classe der K.b. Akademie der Wissenschaften* (Munich, 1873), pp. 695ff. The text of *Ovide moralisé*, discussed on pp. 165ff., is available in five volumes issued by the Royal Dutch Academy in Amsterdam between 1915 and 1938. Pierre Bersuire's *Metamorphosis Ovidiana moraliter . . . explanata* (Paris, 1509), mentioned on p. 166, can be found in Stephen Orgel's Garland edition of 1979.

INDEX

References in **boldface** indicate
major discussion

Abelard, Peter, 2, 83, 163–64
Abortion, 17, 62–63
Achilles, 18, 72, 73–77, 88, 89, 95,
 149
Acis, 28, 160
Acontius, 18
Actaeon, 114, 115
Adonis, 9, 28, 29, 159
Aegeus, 137–38
Aeneas, 10, 18, 34, 43, 91–92, 127–
 28, 159
Aeneid (Vergil): *Amores* and, 63–64;
 Ars Amatoria and, 95; *Fasti* and, 33–
 35; *Metamorphoses* and, 107, 109,
 112, 118–21, 125–29, 132, 143–44
Agamemnon, 4, 18, 73, 74, 76, 97
Agrippa, 37
Alcyone, 9, 160
Amores (Loves), **15–20**, **53–69**; allu-
 sions to, 161, 163–64; *Ars Amatoria*
 and, 25; exile poetry and, 43; *Me-
 dea* and, 20; Ovid's poses in, 5, 58–
 61
Anagnorisis. See Recognition scene
Anchises, 10
Andromache, 74–75, 95–97
Andromeda, 122–24, 126, 162
Anna Perenna, festival of, 33–35
Apollo, 100, 108, 113, 159
Apollodorus, 133
Apollonius of Rhodes, 27, 30
Appearance and reality, 151–54
Arachne, 28, 114
Aratus, 84

Arethusa, 69
Argo, 88
Argus, 165, 166
Ariadne, 18, 71, 138, 140
Ariosto, Ludovico, 99, 163
Ars Amatoria, **23–25**, **83–98**; advice
 in, 83–84; form v. subject in, 87–
 89, 97–98; influence of, 157, 160,
 164; originality of, 93; Ovidian wit
 in, 146–49; psychology and, 3;
 subjects in, 23–25
Art, allusion to Ovid in, 159
Atalanta, 29, 127
Athena. *See* Minerva
Atlas, 122
Augustus (Gaius Julius Caesar Oc-
 tavianus): in *Amores*, 64; in *Ars
 Amatoria*, 92–95; and the arts, 14;
 exile of Ovid by, 35–40; *Metamor-
 phoses* and, 135, 143; morality and,
 36–38, 39, 52; in poems from exile,
 43, 45, 49, 50–52; Roman legend
 and, 36, 38
Aura (breeze), 132
Aurora, 131
Automedon, 88

Bacchus, 115
Bach, J. S., 159–60
Battle, as theme, 118
Battle of Lapiths and Centaurs, 128–
 30, 131, 140
Baucis, 27, 156, 159
Beauty, 22–23, 102, 103
Biographical information, 12, 13–15,
 35–36
Boccaccio, 163

175